THE
BRANDYWINE
BOOK OF THE SEASONS

ELLA & ROGER MORRIS

LondonBritain
PRESS

September 2012

THE BRANDYWINE BOOK OF THE SEASONS

LONDONBRITAIN PRESS
25 MILLSTONE COURT
LANDENBERG, PENNSYLVANIA 19350

Cover and design by Leslie Kedash, Kedash Design.

Also by the authors: **The Brandywine Book of Food** (with Cathleen Ryan), 2009

ISBN 978-1-4675-3951-7

ACKNOWLEDGEMENTS

All books are content-driven, and the content of this book is people—friends and acquaintances who live in the Brandywine region. They have been most patient with us as we have asked questions, taken and re-taken photos and probed them gently, then firmly, to extract their recipes. We genuinely thank them all.

Leslie Kedash has similarly worked patiently with us as we have tried to merge our sense of the kind of book we wanted with Leslie's desire to make it look even more attractive than we could have hoped. Leslie, take a deep bow.

And then there is Roger's brother Ed, who agreed to proof read the pages. His corrections have been apt, and his editorial suggestions have been mostly followed. If you see an error, don't blame Ed.

Finally, we acknowledge the merchants who believed in this book enough to purchase it in volume. They, and we, hope you like it—love it actually—and will want to share copies with your relatives and friends.

Roger and Ella Morris

FOR EVERYTHING, A SEASON

About 30 years ago, we moved into Chester County, Pennsylvania, and in the years since we've been fortunate to become friends with, or to know well, many people who raise animals, grow produce, make wine, craft artisan foods, run restaurants and operate markets.

And we know almost as many amateur cooks who entertain well and know where to send us invitations.

In this book, we introduce you to some of them, take you into their homes and places of business and shamelessly steal their recipes just for you.

In short, The Brandywine region—which we broadly define as southern Chester County and northern Delaware—is a food-lover's haven. But for those of us who live in the Brandywine, it is more than just that. Although home to thousands of people, the land preservation movement is strong here, which means many farms will not become subdivisions, and tracts of unspoiled land will remain under easement.

In addition, if we do yearn for something more urbane, Philadelphia and Baltimore are just a couple of hours away by car, and the same time on Amtrak will get us to New York and Washington.

We invite you to come visit us if you live outside the Brandywine. If you have good food-production and culinary skills we might entice you to stay awhile.

TABLE OF CONTENTS

THE WINTER

AWAKENING TO A SNOWFALL

It came while you slept. You look out the window at the still-darkened morning and you can see nothing but white. Is it still snowing? How much is there? Where did I put the snow shovel?

Winter comes to the Brandywine in two seasons, one for the children, one for adults—and sometimes they merge in our minds.

As soon as Thanksgiving is over, there is something that makes us adults want to congregate, to be with friends on cold evenings. We will have a party. We will take gifts to friends. We will decorate things brightly to protest the drabness of the outdoors—the frigid, even threatening, impersonality of the colorless landscape. We will talk a little louder, perhaps drink a little more, we will have fun!

As soon as Thanksgiving is over, there is something that makes us adults want to congregate, to be with friends on cold evenings.

*A*nd then we will open our souls again to nature's change. We will take the dog for a long walk in the now-open woods. We will rediscover as we drive cross country the traces of the past—a decaying wooden barn in a distant field, the stone foundations of an old farm house, the trench-like outlines of an abandoned mill race. We will check the pond for the thickness of ice.

And we will remember—as we stand by the back door gazing out—the season of children. Whatever happened to that old sled? When was the last time we had a friendly snowball fight? Are we up to building a snowman with the kids or the grandkids? Do we want to break out the cross-country skis?

But it is Saturday morning, it is snowing, and you don't have to go to work. The kid in you gets a big bowl and a big spoon, sets out on the kitchen counter the milk or cream, the vanilla flavoring and the jar of sugar, and you step outside. It is time to make snow cream.

Holidays with the **Morrises**

Most years, when we had family in West Virginia, we would travel there for Thanksgiving and often Christmas, hoping that the lake effect snows wouldn't impede our way as we journeyed through western Maryland. There were never any culinary surprises by either parents—the holidays meant turkey and ham, or, sometimes, ham and turkey.

Although we miss these visits, we do enjoy cooking just for two of us for the holidays—sort of like two kids who snuck off by ourselves. So we automatically take turkey and ham off our menu for the holidays, and, since we're meat eaters and always enjoy game, we often prepare pheasant with a cream sauce or rabbit with a two-mustard sauce.

This year, however, Ella was in the mood for lamb.

We considered lamb chops, which we both love, but instead adapted a recipe we like for stuffed breast of veal. The butcher had a nice-looking butterflied leg of lamb—at 2 pounds just right for two people with one meal of leftovers.

Unlike a veal breast, a butterflied leg has no cavity, so we had to make do by wrapping the spinach-and-pork-sausage stuffing in the middle. It worked fine. We decided on smashed potatoes and asparagus—very simple—to go with it, although Ella found a recipe for an orange marmalade with lemon and smoked paprika to spice up the asparagus.

Now on to the wine!

Although we seldom prepare fish for holidays, we do like a heartier fish dish as a change of pace, and our recipe for salmon steak with a white bean salad makes a very satisfying meal on a cold winter's evening.

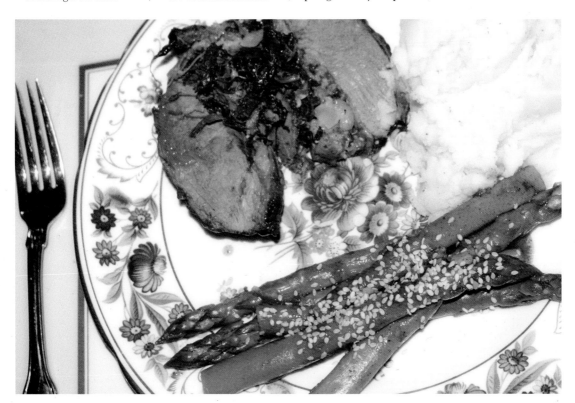

RECIPE

SALMON STEAKS WITH WHITE BEAN SALAD

ROGER & ELLA MORRIS

Adapted from the Tribeca Grill

Serves: 2

INGREDIENTS

¼ cup	chopped celery
¼ cup	chopped scallions
¼ cup	chopped carrots
2 tbsp.	lemon juice
2 tbsp.	herbs de Provence
15 oz. can	cannellini beans, drained except for 2 tbsp. of liquid
olive oil	
2 tsp.	chopped thyme
salt and pepper to taste	
2	6 oz. salmon filets
2 tbsp.	lemon juice
1 cup	small-leafed fresh greens

PREPARATION

1. Drizzle small amount of olive oil in non-stick skillet, add celery, scallions and carrots and cook lightly until tender, about 5 minutes.

2. Add lemon juice, herbs, beans and reserve liquid and cook about 2 minutes, stirring, until heated. Cover to keep warm and set aside.

3. Sprinkle thyme, salt and pepper over fillets and cook in a baking sheet in pre-heated 375 degree oven for 10-15 minutes or until flakey.

4. To assemble, plate fillets, sprinkle with lemon juice and add bean salad around edges. Cover about half the fillet and bean salad with the fresh greens.

STUFFED BUTTERFLIED LEG OF LAMB

ROGER & ELLA MORRIS

We normally fix this recipe with a breast of veal, which is a neater package, but the lamb tastes better to us.

Serves: 2-4

INGREDIENTS

1	medium-size butterflied leg of lamb
2 tbsp.	butter
2 tbsp.	olive oil
1	medium onion chopped
10 oz.	package of cooked spinach, squeezed dry
½ lb.	mild pork sausage
1	egg, beaten
salt and pepper to taste	

PREPARATION

1. Saute the onion in a sauce pan with the olive oil until soft. Stir in and cook the rest of the ingredients until the sausage is done.

2. Spread out the butterfly leg in a greased, large oven pan and put the stuffing mixture along the top of lamb. Where possible, gather up the sides of the leg around the stuffing and tie lightly with cooking twine. Much of the stuffing will be uncovered and falling out the sides. That's okay; this isn't meant to be a neat dish.

3. Bake in an oven pre-heated to 375 degrees for about 2-2 ½ hours or until meat thermometer in thickest bar reads 130-135 degrees (medium rare).

4. Let rest a few minutes, remove and slice, scooping up the excess dressing.

Elegant Dining at **The Orchard**

When food lovers in the Brandywine region want a very elegant place to dine with excellent food to match, they think of The Orchard, located just a few hundred yards west of the entrance to Longwood Gardens along the busily traveled U.S. Route 1.

As it closes in on the completion of its first decade, The Orchard has achieved a reputation of being classy without being stuffy and intimate without being crowded. The atmosphere is one of muted elegance—a flush of fresh flowers, linen table cloths, quiet service. Both the founding owners and the current owner, Chef Gary Trevisani, have cultivated a clientele who appreciate the details. As The Orchard is a BYOB, the staff will collect your bottles at reception and have them ready for decanting within a few minutes of your being seated.

Chef Trevisani's food is fresh, classically prepared and well-presented without being over the top or theatrical. Trevisani came to The Orchard after several years at the Restaurant School at Walnut Hill College, the country's first private college dedicated to careers in fine dining and luxury hospitality businesses. Chef Trevisani eventually guided the curricula at the college as its Director of Culinary Arts.

So pull up a chair as he serves us his recipes for beet and chevre salad and lamb shanks *osso bucco*.

THE ORCHARD | KENNETT SQUARE

WWW.THEORCHARDBYOB.COM

RECIPE

Roasted Baby Beet with Chèvre Salad

Chef Gary Trevisani

Serves: 4 appetizer salads

INGREDIENTS

2 each	baby candy strip beets	**¼ cup**	mesclun greens
2 each	baby golden beets	**¼ cup**	micro greens
2 each	baby red beets	**¼ cup**	white balsamic vinaigrette
2 cloves	garlic	**salt and freshly cracked**	
¼ bunch	thyme	**pepper to taste**	
¼ cup	olive oil	**½ lb.**	smoked bacon,
½ cup	chèvre (goat cheese)		cut into thick strips
2 heads	frisée lettuce		

PREPARATION

1. Remove the tops of all beets, leaving a small amount of stalk on each beet, coat with olive oil and place in roasting pan with the garlic cloves and thyme. Cover with aluminum foil

2. Place in 425 degree oven and roast until the beets are just cooked through. This should take about 35 to 45 minutes. Remove from the oven and cool.

3. Once cooled, remove the skin from the beets and cut each beet in half. Place beets in a container until ready to serve.

4. Place chèvre in a bowl. Using two spoons, shape chèvre into quenelles and hold until ready to serve.

5. Clean and dry the frisée and set aside. Have the mesclun greens and micro greens ready to serve.

6. Gently toss the frisée with the white balsamic vinaigrette and season. Do the same with the mesclun mix. (I like to keep this separate for plating purposes.)

7. On a large plate arrange the beets with the cut side up, then arrange the chèvre around the plate using three quenelles. Arrange the frisée and the mesclun greens on plate in a decorative fashion.

8. Lightly heat the bacon and arrange on plate along with the micro green for final decoration.

LAMB SHANKS OSSO BUCCO STYLE WITH ISRAELI COUCOUS AND ORANGE FENNEL SAUCE

CHEF GARY TREVISANI

Serves: 4

INGREDIENTS

3 tbsp.	olive oil		**2 tbsp.**	fennel seeds
8	lamb shanks cut into osso bucco style		**2 tbsp.**	black peppercorns
			2 tbsp.	bay leaves
I large	onion, sliced		**2 cups**	cooked Israeli couscous
I head	fennel, sliced		**2 tbsp.**	olive oil
5 cloves	garlic, sliced		**2 tbsp.**	harissa sauce
I quart	chicken stock		**10**	zucchini, tournée cut
I cup	tomatoes, chopped		**I tbsp.**	butter
2 zest	oranges		**fennel fronds**	
5 each	star anise		**2 tsp.**	orange powder

PREPARATION

1. Heat olive oil in braiser.

2. Season the lamb shanks with salt and pepper on both sides and place in braiser. Brown both sides, then remove from braiser.

3. Place onions and fennel in braiser and cook until softened. Add the garlic and cook for a minute or two.

4. Return the lamb to the braiser and half cover with the chicken stock. Add the tomatoes, orange zest, star anise, fennel seeds, black peppercorns and bay leaves.

5. Bring to a boil then turn to a bare simmer. Cook this very slowly until the meat is very tender. Once meat is cooked, cool in braising liquid, strain and reserve the braising liquid. (Braised lamb shanks will hold up to 4 days in refrigerator.)

6. Heat lamb shanks in some of the braising liquid until heated through.

7. Heat braising liquid in sauce pan and reduce liquid until just thickened. Away from the heat, add whole butter and whisk.

8. Heat the couscous in some olive oil and the harissa until hot.

9. Heat the zucchini in olive oil and season with salt and pepper.

10. Pour sauce onto heated plate, then place portion of harissa couscous in the center. Place two shanks on the couscous and then garnish with the zucchini. Serve immediately.

The Larneds and the Art of Living

David Larned and Sarah Lamb are two young professional artists who spend most of their days laboring in front of an easel in their side-by-side studios in an outbuilding of an old farmhouse near West Chester. It's not surprising that they love to entertain on weekends.

Although both are well-rounded in their artistic abilities, David makes a living painting portraits, while Sarah specializes in still lifes—often of food—and landscapes carried in galleries in New York and Houston. With her roots in Virginia and Georgia, many of her dishes are updates of family recipes. David likes to hunt for game and to concentrate on the wines being served.

And to make their entertaining even more special, they live with their two-year-old daughter Sadie and their pug Weezie in a historic house that once belonged to the actor Claude Rains—which they have updated and decorated to fit their tastes. Their lovely paintings are everywhere.

We visited them one winter's afternoon, while there was a skift of snow still fresh on the ground from the previous night's flurry, stopping along the way for a gift of a fresh, rosemary-scented boule from the ladies at Red Lion bakery.

At the door, we were greeted by the smells of Sarah's Brunswick stew—a special stew because it was an adaptation of a family recipe and because David had provided the quail for the pot from a hunting trip in Georgia. While waiting for the stew to finish, we sampled Sarah's delicious Brandywine Alexanders and watched Weezie follow the toddling Sadie through the house, hoping that a morsel of food would be dropped to the floor—as it often was.

DAVID LARNED & SARAH LAMB | WEST CHESTER
www.davidlarned.com | www.sarahlamb.net

RECIPE

Brunswick Stew
with Quail and Crispy Pancetta

Sarah Lamb

"For the crispy pancetta—Get the butcher to very thinly slice about 25 pieces of pancetta. Place in a single layer in a flat pan into a 450 degree oven for about 10 minutes, watching to make sure they don't burn."

Serves: 4-6

INGREDIENTS

3-4 lbs.	quail, dressed and split (roughly 6-8 quail) Chicken can be substituted
1 ½ tsp.	salt
1	onion quartered
2-3	pieces of bacon
3	14 oz. cans diced tomatoes
2 cups	butter beans
2 cups	corn
2	russet potatoes, thinly sliced
1 ½ - 2 cups	chicken broth
1 tbsp.	sugar
1 cup	diced onion
¼ - ½ cup	smoky bbq sauce (I prefer Stubbs)

FOR TOPPING:

1	handful chopped parsley
25	pieces thinly sliced pancetta, crisped in the oven

PREPARATION

1. Simmer the first four ingredients for 1 ½ -2 hours until the meat falls easily off the bone. Strain the broth and save.

2. Pick the meat off the quail and put aside.

3. Add remaining ingredients to the quail broth and cook until the veggies are tender—about 2 hours.

4. Add the quail to the pot. Season to taste with salt, pepper (and more sugar if needed)

5. Ladle the stew into bowls and top with parsley and pancetta. (I like a few dashes of Tabasco in mine.)

"The BBQ sauce was a last minute addition in homage to my Georgia roots."

Brandywine Alexanders

Sarah Lamb

"I prefer Häagen Daz to other high-end vanilla ice creams. I think there's more milk fat in it, and it makes the shake smooth and creamy."

Serves: 6

INGREDIENTS

1 quart	vanilla ice cream
8 oz.	brandy
4 oz.	creme de cacao

PREPARATION

1. Put everything into a blender and blend until smooth.

2. I like to put mine back in the freezer for a few hours and take it out right before serving.

3. Pour into Brandy snifters and top with ground nutmeg and pirouette cookie.

New Times at **Domaine Hudson**

I remember visiting Tom Hudson a few years ago at the new restaurant he was creating near Wilmington's Washington Street Bridge. The wine bar was in place, but the wall coverings were still going up, and opening night was just a few days away. The place was a mess.

But Domaine Hudson did open on time and to great critical success as a sophisticated downtown restaurant with small and large plates and excel-lent wines by the glass in three sizes that would have pleased Goldy and the Bears.

In time, beers were added to the wines, and occasionally a cock-tail might appear.

Times change.

Tom decided last year that the restaurant business had been fun but that he wanted to move on. Literally. Not long after he sold it to Mike and Beth Ross, he started construction on a house in Jamaica with a veranda on which he could drink rum—his newest passion—and determine if those were beautiful sunrises or sunsets. Or both.

Mike Ross is a lover of food and wine and a veterinarian who teaches at the University of Penn-sylvania's New Bolton Center at Unionville. So, when I visited the restaurant earlier in the year just before dinner, equine paintings were be-ing installed on the walls at Domaine Hudson.

The transition between owners has been seamless, in part because of a spar-kling young chef named J.D. Morton. The week after J.D. gave us these recipes for tuna confit and for monkfish and creamy leeks, he was nominated at 24 as a finalist in the James Beard competition for Rising Star Chef.

Let's raise a glass to Tom, to Mike and Beth and to J.D.

DOMAINE HUDSON | WILMINGTON

www.domainehudson.com

RECIPE

Tuna Confit with Soy Ginger Marinade

Chef J.D. Morton

Serves: 4

INGREDIENTS

12 oz.	tuna belly or loin
1 cup	toasted chopped almonds
½ cup	water chestnuts
¼ cup	finely chopped scallions
2 tbsp.	toasted sesame seeds
2 cups	canola oil (enough to cover tuna)
2	crushed garlic cloves
1	thai chile split or 1 tsp. of red chili flake
1 head	Boston bibb lettuce

FOR THE MARINADE:

¾ cup	Hoisin sauce	**1 tbsp.**	lime juice
2 tbsp.	soy sauce	**½ tsp.**	lime zest
1	garlic clove, finely chopped	**¼ tsp.**	salt
1	shallot, finely chopped	**½ tsp.**	sesame oil
		1 tsp.	grated ginger

PREPARATION

1.   Set oven to 350 degrees. Place tuna in an oven-proof dish and cover with oil and add crushed garlic and chili.

2.   Place on stove top over medium heat until oil begins to slightly bubble, then place in oven for 25 minutes.

3.   Once cooked place the tuna (in oil) in the refrigerator until cool.

4.   To make marinade, add all ingredients in a small bowl and mix.

5.   In another large bowl, add almonds, chestnuts, scallions, and sesame seeds.

6.   Remove tuna from oil and add 1 tbsp. of the cooking oil into the large bowl. Shred the tuna by hand and add it to the large bowl. Add all marinade to large bowl and stir to combine.

7.   Pull individual leaves off head of lettuce and fill each with 3 oz. of tuna mix. Garnish with chopped carrot and more sesame seeds.

MONKFISH WITH CREAMY LEEKS

CHEF J.D. MORTON

Serves: 4

INGREDIENTS

4	6 oz. monkfish filets
I tbsp.	unsalted butter
2 tbsp.	canola oil
4 sprigs	thyme

FOR THE CREAMY LEEKS:

3	leeks
I tbsp.	butter
¼ cup	heavy cream
I tsp.	mustard powder
¼ tsp.	cayenne pepper

FOR THE BLACK GARLIC PUREE:

I head	black garlic
¼ cup	chicken stock/broth
I	shallot

FOR THE GREEN PEPPERCORN SAUCE:

I tbsp.	green peppercorns
I cup	chicken stock/broth
½ cup	white wine
I	garlic clove, chopped
I	shallot, chopped
2 sprigs	thyme
I	bay leaf
I oz.	parsley stems
I ½ tbsp.	butter

continued on page 28

Monkfish with Creamy Leeks...continued from page 27

PREPARATION

Preheat oven to 350 degrees.

1.   To make the creamy leeks, cut the very green tops off leeks and root end. Split the leeks in half and slice into half-moons and rinse well under cool water to remove grit. Melt the butter in a small pot and add leeks, a pinch of salt, mustard powder and cayenne pepper. Cook until leeks are tender, then add cream and reduce by half. Reserve leeks in a warm place.

2.   To make the black garlic puree, sweat the shallot in a small amount of canola oil, add black garlic cloves and chicken stock. Cook for 5 minutes and puree in blender.

3.   To make the green peppercorn sauce, sweat the garlic and shallot in the ½ tbsp. of butter. Add white wine and reduce by half. Add green peppercorns and chicken stock. Wrap the herbs in cheese cloth and tie with butcher's twine then place in pot. Reduce the sauce by ¾. Once reduced, move sauce to a saute pan (discard the herbs) over no heat and swirl in the remaining butter.

4.   To assemble the dish, put a pan over medium high heat with the 1 tbsp. of oil until shimmering. Add monkfish filets and sear, then add the butter and thyme sprigs and baste the fish filets for 2 minutes. Flip the filets and place in oven for 8 minutes. After putting the fish in the oven, gently reheat the other components over low heat. To finish assembly, put the black garlic puree on the plate in a smear fashion or a small circle. Place 3 ounces of leeks on top of puree, then the monkfish on top of the leeks and, finally, put 1 tsp. of the green peppercorn sauce along the fish making sure to get a few peppercorns on the plate.

Lighting the Tree with the Schaers

Thomas and Barbara Dallap Schaer live in the cutting-edge world of modern animal medicine at the University of Pennsylvania and at its New Bolton Center for large animals near Unionville. Although they have various duties at Penn, Barbara works primarily as surgeon for large animals, which normally means horses but has included animals that have run away from the circus, while Tom is more heavily involved in research, including spinal medicine that may eventually have human applications.

But for all of that, they come home to their farm in Landenberg and their daughters, Ale (pronounced "Al-ee") and Julia, a flock of around 35 sheep, chickens, more than 25 hives or colonies of bees, numerous cats and dogs as well as a wandering peacock. And tradition reigns here at the old stone farm house whose wide fireplace is often ablaze on winter evenings.

Tom grew up in Switzerland where his family had a farm, and he and Barbara, from western Pennsylvania, are farmers at heart. Their herd of East Friesian and Lacaune sheep at the Schaer's 30-acre, 250-year-old Meadowset Farm & Apiary is raised for their meat, wool, milk and cheese (a commercial cheese barn is in the works). The small valley in which the farm sits in often a-jangle to the Swiss bells most of the sheep wear as they move from field to field.

It is at Christmas, however, that tradition truly reigns. The Schaers cut their tall tree on Christmas Eve and decorate it with candles from Switzerland which Tom ceremoniously lights as the girls wait for presents while being read stories in English and German by Barbara.

MEADOWSET FARM & APIARY | LANDENBERG

RECIPE

TRADITIONAL GRASS-FED POT ROAST

BARBARA DALLAP SCHAER

Serves: 4

INGREDIENTS

2 tbsp.	unsalted butter
2	carrots, chopped medium
2	celery stalks, chopped medium
1	shallot, chopped medium
1	small onion, thinly sliced
8 oz.	shitake mushrooms, sliced
8 oz.	white mushrooms, sliced
1 cup	red wine
1 cup	porcini stock
2 tbsp.	tomato paste
3 lb.	grass-fed chuck roast
1-2 tbsp.	good quality white balsamic vinegar

PREPARATION

1.   Saute onions, shallot, carrots, celery, and mushrooms in unsalted butter and some olive oil. Cook until softened and fragrant, about 8-10 minutes.

2.   Add red wine, scraping up any browned bits on the bottom of the pan. After wine has decreased in volume by about half, add porcini stock (or decent beef or vegetable stock, if porcini is unavailable) and tomato paste; mix well.

3.   Place chuck roast in center of vegetables, and bring stock to a simmer.

4.   Place in preheated 325 degree oven and cook until meat is fork tender, and just starting to fall off bone.

5.   Remove roasted meat from vegetables and cover, allowing to rest for about 10-15 minutes before slicing.

6.   Drain excess fat off top of vegetable mix using either gravy separator or spoon. Using hand blender, puree vegetables until smooth. (If desired, whisk about 1 tbsp flour into small volume of gravy mixture, then add to remainder of gravy.) Warm gently over low heat, stirring to thicken.

7.   Off heat, add splash of good quality white balsamic vinegar, and season to taste.

8.   Slice meat about ¼" thick; serve with gravy.

RISOTTO
WITH GRASS-FED FILET MIGNON, TOASTED WALNUTS AND DOLCE GORGONZOLA

BARBARA DALLAP SCHAER

Serves: 4

INGREDIENTS

3 tbsp.	olive oil, extra virgin
1	medium yellow onion, finely chopped
2 cloves	garlic, finely chopped or pressed through garlic press
1 ½ cups	Arborio rice
1 cup	red wine
4 cups	good quality stock (porcini, chicken, vegetable), heated and kept warm
3 oz.	gorgonzola, dolce if available
2 tsp.	finely chopped tarragon, plus sprigs for garnish
½ cup	walnuts, lightly toasted
4	petite grass-fed filets mignon

PREPARATION

1. Gently warm stock for risotto, keeping warm on stove top or low-heat burner.

2. Salt and pepper filets on both sides, and allow to come to room temperature while you are cooking risotto.

3. Saute onions in olive oil until soft and translucent. Add Arborio rice, and heat while stirring until only a small white dot remains in the center.

4. Add wine, and heat thoroughly while stirring until volume of wine decreases by about half. Begin adding the stock, one ladleful at a time while stirring, until rice has absorbed most of the liquid.

5. Continue adding stock in this manner until rice is creamy and has softened but remains slightly firm in the center (about 30 minutes). When there is about 2 cups of stock remaining, add tarragon to stock and continue to add. Reserve about ¼ cup for finishing risotto.

6. When risotto is about half way through, pan sear filets to desired degree of doneness, remove from heat and cover, allowing to rest before slicing.

7. Remove risotto from heat and gently stir in gorgonzola.

8. Spoon risotto into shallow bowls or pasta dishes, top with walnuts, tarragon sprigs, and sliced filet mignon. Serve immediately.

Susan Cooks, **Linda Pours**

As soon as the last days of November fly off the calendar, we begin to think of seasonal parties when festivities match the giddiness of those of June at the other end of the calendar.

And some of the people we know are natural party-givers.

Two such people are Susan Teiser and Linda Collier, longtime friends, longtime owners of small, complementary businesses and longtime collaborators when it comes to food and drink. Susan cooks. Linda pours.

Susan is owner of the Centreville Café and Montrachet Fine Foods in Centreville, and Linda is owner of Collier's of Centreville, a wine shop a few doors up the road from Susan's café. The two collaborate on wine classes and wine dinners, so it seemed only natural this past season when Linda celebrated her 30th anniversary as a wine purveyor that they jointly throw a party.

We received our invitation for the event, and, of course, accepted and showed up at the café just before the guy playing bagpipes, who may or may not have been invited to keen the night way. While Susan and her staff brought out round after round of hot and cold party food from the open kitchen, Linda and her staff poured glass after glass of her favorite wine—the kind that has bubbles.

And so it went, and so it goes—parties before Hanukkah and Christmas, parties to celebrate Hanukkah and Christmas and parties to welcome in the New Year.

CENTREVILLE CAFÉ | CENTREVILLE
www.centrevillecafe.com

COLLIER'S OF CENTREVILLE | CENTREVILLE
www.collierswine.com

BABY POTATOES
TOPPED WITH CAVIAR

CHEF SUSAN TEISER

"You can also add a dash of hot sauce, lemon zest or minced shallot if desired to the sour cream and chives."

Serves: 48

INGREDIENTS

24	very small red or blue potatoes
8 oz.	sour cream, crème fraiche or Greek yogurt
2 oz.	fresh chives, snipped into very small pieces
2 ½ oz.	good quality paddlefish caviar

PREPARATION

1. Wash potatoes and cut in half.

2. Take each half and scoop out small amount from middle of the flat side with melon-balling tool. Then cut a small slice off the round side of each so the potato will sit flat.

3. Place potatoes flat side down on non-stick baking sheet and roast 20-30 minutes in 300 degree oven until done. Set aside to cool.

4. Combine sour cream and chives and set aside.

5. When cool, arrange potatoes on serving tray. Spoon small amount of sour cream into each scooped-out hole and top with caviar.

6. Serve chilled.

LOBSTER AGNOLOTTI

CHEF SUSAN TEISER

*"If using fresh lobster, the claws and knuckles
have more flavor than the tails."*

Serves: 12-16

INGREDIENTS

1 lb.	thin fresh pasta sheets (thinnest setting if homemade)
2 lbs.	fresh or frozen lobster meat
6 tbsp.	butter, unsalted at room temperature
¼ cup	flat-leaf parsley, minced
½ tsp.	black pepper
1	egg white, well-whisked

FOR SERVING:

1	cantaloupe, halved

PREPARATION

1. Chop lobster into ¼ in. or smaller pieces and place in stainless mixing bowl.

2. Mix other ingredients together and add to lobster meat.

3. Cut the pasta into small squares (about 2") on a lightly floured board. Put 1 tsp. of the lobster filling on each square.

4. Brush edges of each square with egg white and squeeze into small purses. Arrange on baking sheet and freeze overnight.

5. Cook the pursed squares 2-3 minutes in lightly salted water and drain. With frilled toothpicks arrange on an upside-down cantaloupe half (see photo) and serve immediately.

THE SPRING

CONTEMPLATING OUR 'DO LISTS'

Spring awakens us. We must prepare our "do lists."
The smell of the warming earth calls to us to dig up the garden and
hope the tomatoes and squash do better this year.

We must get into an exercise program before we bare ourselves at the beach.

We get the desire to take long walks, even if we have nowhere to go and no place to be.

The garage needs cleaning out. Or the basement. Or the attic.

Then there is our love-hate relation with the lawn. We need to buy grass seed
for those bare spots, but secretly hope that it doesn't grow too quickly.

Does anyone think, as the energy surges within us, to stop and smell the daffodils?

We begin shedding layers: a coat, a jacket, a sweater, until we are back to T shirts.

Spring means baseball, but we no longer seriously think about playing it.

The smell of the warming earth calls to us to dig up the garden and hope the tomatoes and squash do better this year.

So, check the schedule to see when the Blue Rocks open at Frawley Stadium.

And while we are thinking about being social, do we want to get a group of friends together for a picnic at one of the point-to-point races?

We need to feel fresh air, so we rush the season by driving the convertible with the top down, windows up, and the heat full blast. And we further rush the season by eating outside at the local café, even if the April wind is still cold.

Let's toss out the old grill onto the waste heap and buy a new one, maybe even go back to using charcoal.

As we drive to work behind a school bus, we think it won't be long before it's parked for the summer. Who do we know that is graduating? Don't you wish we were kids again and could play marbles?

And, as we go to bed, exhausted by the contemplation of our list, we think it's about time to set the clock forward for another year.

Springtime **Chez Roger & Ella**

We both like to cook. Ella is more practical and has better skills, while Roger is more experimental. We have also been very practical as to who cooks and who cleans. For years, Roger was the executive chef when Ella had to commute daily to New York. Now that Roger is on the road more, writing about people who make wine, Ella does most of the cooking.

We both like to entertain, which, these days, means more dinners for six or eight and fewer big parties—except when we have a new book to launch or Ella is celebrating a new art exhibit. Nevertheless, we find ourselves eating out more with one or two couples, which means no one has to clean up. Is it a New Age or is it Old Age?

Through the years, we have had a number of friends who are chefs and who no one thinks (or dares) to invite to their homes for dinner. We think of these as ideal Monday-night dinners, as that is usually the night commercial chefs have off. We are way too smart to try to dazzle them with virtuoso dishes—there is no way we can match their skills—but we do like to have at least one course be daring in its combination of ingredients. The idea is to entertain them with something they might not have had but never try to challenge them. Besides, having good wine helps to smooth over any culinary inadequacies.

When we eat inside, we always have candles and good music and wine. But now that it's spring, we start to eat out on deck more often, and our yard cats come running when they smell beef or fish or chicken on the grill.

They are perhaps our harshest and most-honest critics—more so than our foodie or chef friends. Over-spice a dish, and they walk away from the table scraps we put down for them with obvious disdain for our menu planning.

RECIPE

CHICKEN SALTIMBOCCA

ELLA MORRIS

Serves: 4

INGREDIENTS

4	skinless chicken breasts, pounded flat
flour for dredging	
4 tbsp.	olive oil
2 tbsp.	butter
½ cup	grated cheese, such as Asiago
8	thin slices prosciutto or other ham
I cup	dry white wine
2 tbsp.	minced fresh sage
salt and pepper to taste	
4	whole sage leaves for garnish

PREPARATION

1. Preheat oven to 375 degrees.

2. Dredge breasts in flour, shaking off excess, and sauté until brown in olive oil in large skillet over medium-high heat, turning once.

3. Keep oil and juices in skillet while transferring breasts to shallow baking pan. Sprinkle cheese evenly over breasts, then fold over two slices of prosciutto per breast.

4. Bake until chicken is thoroughly done, about 10 minutes.

5. Meanwhile, add the butter, wine and chopped sage to the skillet and deglaze to make a sauce.

6. Transfer chicken to platter or individual plates, drizzle on the sauce and add a fresh sage leaf to each breast.

STACKED EGG CREPES, JEAN LOUIS

RECIPE

ROGER MORRIS

We once served these at our runners parties as the centerpiece with glasses of Champagne. It looks simple, but is difficult to assemble. The recipe is from John-Louis Palladin, late chef of the Watergate restaurant in Washington, D.C. It consists of 15 layers. You can do fewer (or more.)

Serves: About 12-16 as appetizers

INGREDIENTS

3 doz.   fresh eggs, beaten
15   different flavorings, such as spices, meats, cheeses, vegetables, about two tablespoons each, finely diced, for everything but spices, about ½ to 1 teaspoon each
lots of olive oil
salt and pepper to taste
1 cup   fresh or canned tomato sauce

PREPARATION

1. First experiment with a very small, shallow skillet to see what the best assembly method is for you. The idea is to barely cook one ladle of eggs in a little olive oil, then stack each layer, one by one. The challenge is to slide or flip over each layer so that it lands flat and even on top of the previous one.

2. Once you've perfected your technique, brush the skillet with olive oil over medium heat and put in one small ladle of eggs. Quickly sprinkle over one of the ingredients, such as ham or diced hot peppers.

3. Don not turn the mixture! Once almost done, transfer first layer to a serving plate with a rim (it gets juicy).

4. Continue layer upon layer until completed. A few minor folds and tears don't matter if they are down in the stack.

5. Invert a plate on top of the stack—the plate has to be big enough to overlap on all sides—and wrap the whole thing lightly in plastic wrap. Place in the refrigerator overnight with a large can of peaches or something sufficiently heavy to help condense the stack.

6. Next day, remove from fridge, wipe away the juices that have drained out, trim the edges with a knife for uniformity and serve. Each slice will be like geological strata.

7. Serve small slices on individual plates with a good drizzle of tomato sauce. Champagne optional.

Everyone's **Bistro on the Corner**

Mickey Donatello runs the kind of neighborhood restaurant that makes you want to move to his neighborhood. The bar calls you to linger for one more sip and one more story, and the food is casual but not something you will easily find elsewhere. Mickey still lives in the world where he might get sticker shock if he had to put $25 next to an entrée on his menu, the current one topping out at $21.

But that description comes with a curse as well. "Downtown Wilmington is 10 minutes away," Donatello says as he takes five during a busy lunch hour at his Corner Bistro at the intersection of Route 202 and Silverside Road in the Talleyville neighborhood, "but if I'm talking with someone in Trolley Square, they act as if we're way out in the country."

For those of us who live 35 minutes away in Landenberg, we can only apologize for not being able to drop by more often, as we chew on a heavenly tarte flambee ("don't call it a pizza") and dip into a crab and asparagus gratin. "I came across the tarte at a restaurant in New York," Mickey says, "and decided to do some research." He found out they are a specialty of Alsace, and a key to them is the flaky pastry crust that is nowhere like the Italian cousin. Ours is the traditional tarte with goat cheese, lardons and carmelized onions that cry out for a crisp Pinot Gris.

Mickey has recently "tarted up" his restaurant, feeling that the décor and the kitchen needed upgrading after nine years in the business.

Drive by and drop in. You'll want to linger a while.

THE CORNER BISTRO | WILMINGTON
WWW.MYBISTRO.COM

RECIPE

ASPARAGUS & CRAB GRATIN

CHEF MICKEY DONATELLO

Serves: 1

INGREDIENTS

1½ oz.	lump crab meat
6	grilled asparagus spears
2 oz.	mornay sauce (recipe below)
1 oz.	shredded parmesan cheese
2 oz.	panko bread crumbs

PREPARATION

1. Heat oven to 450 degrees.

2. Place grilled asparagus in an individual-serving, oven-safe bowl. Place crab meat in center, top with mornay sauce, bread crumbs and cheese.

3. Bake at 450 degrees for 5-7 minutes, or until bubbly and golden brown.

MORNAY SAUCE INGREDIENTS

2 cups	whole milk
4 tbsp.	pale roux
2 tbsp.	butter
2 oz.	finely minced onion
1 sprig	thyme
1	bay leaf
4 oz.	parmesan cheese
salt and white pepper to taste	
½ tsp.	nutmeg

PREPARATION OF MORNAY SAUCE

1. In a skillet, sweat onion in butter until translucent.

2. Add the milk, thyme, bay leaf, salt and pepper. Bring to a simmer.

3. Whisk in the roux and simmer until smooth (about 10 minutes.)

4. Turn off heat, add parmesan and nutmeg. Strain and hold for service.

TRADITIONAL TART FLAMBÉ

RECIPE

CHEF MICKEY DONATELLO

Serves: 2 to 4

TARTE FLAMBÉ DOUGH (2 12-INCH SHELLS) INGREDIENTS

1 tsp.	instant or rapid-rise yeast
3 cups	(about 14 oz.) all-purpose or bread flour, plus more as needed
2 tsp.	salt
2 tbsp. plus 1 tsp. olive oil	

PREPARATION OF TARTE FLAMBÉ DOUGH

1. Combine yeast, flour and salt in food processor. Turn machine on, and add 1 cup water and 2 tbsp. oil while mixing. Process for about 30 seconds, adding more water through feed tube, a little at a time, until mixture forms a ball and is slightly sticky to the touch. If it is dry, add another tablespoon or two of water, and process for another 10 seconds.

2. Turn dough onto floured work surface, and knead by hand for a few seconds to form a smooth, round ball.

3. Grease bowl with remaining olive oil, and place dough in it. Cover with plastic wrap or damp cloth, and let rise in warm, draft-free area until dough just about doubles in size, or at least 1 hour. (You can also let dough rise more slowly, in refrigerator, for as long as 6 or 8 hours.)

4. Using a rolling pin, roll dough as thin as possible, the thinner the better. Fold edges up and over to form a ridge around the perimeter of the shell. It helps the dough stick better if you rub a little water around the edge beforehand.

5. Pre heat oven to 500 degrees.

TOPPING INGREDIENTS

3 oz.	goat cheese (crumbled)
1	white or yellow onion (sliced thin and caramelized)
3 oz.	thick-cut bacon (diced and cooked in a hot pan ahead of time)

PREPARATION OF TOPPING

1. When oven is hot, spread your toppings over the dough and place the two tarts in the oven for about 6-8 minutes.

2. When the edges of the dough are lightly browned, it's done.

The Bakers at Red Lion

For years we had passed by the old house between E Street and Doe Run roads on our way to friends' houses nearby or to visit what was once Folly Hill Winery and is now Galer Estate, often noticing the French tricolor waving in the breeze but paying scant attention to the sign that seemed to come and go.

Then one day we went inside and were totally enveloped by the smells of baking, especially those of rosemary boules, those classic French rounded loaves, which had just been pulled from the oven across the counter. When we were given a sample bit with fresh butter, we were in love, and we knew we would never pass by again if the sign for fresh bread was out.

Barbara Churchville and Nancy Fenstermacher have been making a few loaves of bread for friends, neighbors and clueful passersby for 21 years. Neither were trained as bakers. "We were married, we had husbands, we had to cook," Barbara explains.

Barbara is the one with the classic and cute eye glasses that look like the headlights on a Ford Model T, and Nancy is the one with the slow but generous smile.

Over the course of the years, their repertoire of breads and sweets has grown to a dozen or so different goodies—anything-but-plain loaves, baguettes, oatmeal bread. These days, Nancy makes most of the sweet rolls—her hot-crossed buns are to cry for—while Barbara does the baking of loafs, preferring not to deal with sweet dough. "It sticks to your hands," she exclaims.

So if you pass by and the sign to their back-door bakery is out, stop by to drop some money in the can—they use the farm-stand honor system—and take away some yeastful, fresh-baked bread. Your car will reward you will lovely aromas for days.

THE BAKERS AT RED LION

327 E. STREET ROAD, KENNETT SQUARE

BREAD PUDDING

NANCY FENSTERMACHER

Serves: 4

INGREDIENTS

3-5 cups	French bread and cinnamon raisin bread, pulled apart, rather large chunks
3 cups	whole milk
¼ - ½ cups	melted butter
½ - ¾ cups	sugar
2-3	eggs beaten
1½ tsp.	cinnamon
1 tsp.	nutmeg
salt to taste	

PREPARATION

1.   Place bread into baking dish (about 3-quart size) and set aside. Warm oven to 350 degrees.

2.   Scald the milk with butter and sugar until all melted.

3.   When cooled slightly, add 2 eggs beaten with salt, cinnamon and nutmeg.

4.   Add liquids to bread in bowl and stir slightly to allow bread to soak.

5.   Place bowl in pan of boiling water so it comes up outside of bowl at least an inch. Bake until knife inserted ½ inch from edge comes out clean, about 40-50 minutes.

6.   Remove from water bath. Can be served warm or cold.

OATMEAL BREAD

RECIPE

BARBARA CHURCHVILLE

*"Great for morning toast with jam or marmalade with
a cup of coffee or tea."*

Yields: 2 loaves

INGREDIENTS

6 cups	flour	**2 cups**	boiling water
2 ½ tsp.	salt	**3 tbsp.**	yeast
2 tbsp.	butter	**⅓ cup**	warm water
½ cup	honey	**egg white for wash**	
I cup	rolled oats	**sea salt to taste**	
½ cup	steel-cut oats		

PREPARATION

I.   Pour boiling water over honey, oats and butter. Add salt and stir. Let cool to lukewarm

2.   Add 3 packages of yeast to ⅓ cup warm water to proof.

3.   Put liquid ingredients in large mixing bowl, add water with yeast, stir slightly to mix. Add flour 2 cups at a time and stir. Add 2 cups more until soft, slightly sticky dough forms.

4.   Turn onto floured surface and knead for 2-5 minutes, adding more flour to keep dough soft and not too firm.

5.   Place in buttered bowl, turn to coat both sides, cover and let rise until doubled, but no more than one hour maximum.

6.   Butter or spray with non-stick oil 2 bread pans 9" long x 3"wide x 5" deep.

7.   Turn out on to lightly floured work surface and cut in to two pieces. Knead each to form a pleasing loaf shape. Place each in a pan, seam side down, pinching seams together.

8.   Slash (not cut down into) top surface with knife in parallel diagonals or diagonal crisscross pattern to allow bread to vent while baking. Brush with egg white wash, sprinkle with cracked sea salt if desired.

9.   Let rise until doubled, then place in pre-heated oven at 425 degrees for I0 minutes. Open door to check. Reduce heat to 375 degrees for 20-30 minutes until pleasingly golden brown on top.

10.   Remove from pans when done, let sit on side till cool.

Terry Peach's Catch

When we did a magazine article on Terry Peach a few years back, we summed up his lifestyle in a few words:

As best I can figure it, Peach, a former tennis tour pro and now flyfishing pro, has three professional missions in his current life, all of them about fishing. One is to conduct flyfishing classes, tie flies, and sell equipment in his Centreville shop, A Marblehead Flyfisher. A second is to guide amateurs like me to where fish are jumping and teach us to get them to bite. Finally, whenever he can break free, he likes a busman's holiday with his buddies—flyfishing 24/7 anyplace on the continent with a couple of feet of water, whether it's ocean surf or mountain stream.

Terry is still a fullthrottle flyfisherman, but he is also newly married—to attorney Mary Ann Plankinton, who owns an organic produce farm, Down to Earth Organics. They both love to cook, and so we visited them for a Sunday morning brunch at their old stone farmhouse in Chadds Ford a few minutes from Terry's Centreville shop.

When we drove up, he was already casting a few shrimp and some fresh tuna steaks on the barbie while Mary Ann and her twin nieces worked on assembling the base for a salad Nicoise while also putting together a Scallops Carry Le Rouet. "My family is from the Rhone Valley," Mary Ann says, "and I still visit relatives every year or two. In fact, I named the scallops dish after their home town—Carry Le Rouet."

As for Terry, the seafood for the salad was not netted by him— he's strictly a catch and release flyfisher.

A MARBLEHEAD FLYFISHER
CENTREVILLE

RECIPE

GRILLED SEAFOOD SALAD NICOISE

MARY ANN PLANKINTON AND TERRY PEACH

"This is a Mediterranean classic made fresh with grilled, seared tuna, shrimp and scallops."

Serves: 4-6 as lunch

INGREDIENTS

2 ½ lbs.	tuna steaks cut I inch thick
8	large sea scallops
8	jumbo shrimp
I head	Boston lettuce, chopped or pulled apart
I lb.	small potatoes, cooked
½ cup	Nicoise olives
½ lb.	haricots verts trimmed, cooked al dente
I pint	grape tomatoes, halved
2	hard-boiled eggs, quartered

INGREDIENTS FOR DRESSING

⅓ cup	extra virgin olive oil
3 tbsp.	fresh lemon juice (try Meyer's)
2 tbsp.	chopped capers in brine
I tbsp.	grainy mustard
I tsp.	anchovy paste
½ tsp.	freshly ground black pepper
pinch	raw sugar
¼ tsp.	kosher salt

PREPARATION

1. Make dressing and marinade by whisking together ingredients

2. Rub the tuna, scallops and shrimp with 3 tbsp. of dressing and grill over high heat for about 4 minutes and transfer to cutting board.

3. Toss the vegetables with the remaining dressing and transfer to serving platter.

4. Slice the tuna and place atop the salad ingredients along with the scallops and shrimps. Top with the quartered eggs and serve.

We serve with a loaf of French bread baked by the Red Lion Bakers and a glass of Bogle, our favorite Pinot Noir.

Scallops Carry Le Rouet

RECIPE

Mary Ann Plankinton and Terry Peach

"This is a dish that may be served as an appetizer or main course. You will need small baking pans with a spring/removable bottom to shape the three-layer individual tarts."

Serves: 4

INGREDIENTS

1	garden-picked zucchini sliced very thin
4	garden picked tomatoes (heirloom if available) chopped
12	large sea scallops, each sliced into 3 thin layers. (I ask the fish monger to slice the scallops for me.)

extra-virgin olive oil for marinade
salt and pepper to taste

PREPARATION

1. Marinate the scallops in extra virgin olive oil, salt and pepper.

2. Sauté the sliced zucchini in olive oil for 2 minutes and set aside.

3. Sauté the chopped tomato until tender, about 4 minutes.

4. Arrange the layers in the individual pans: first the zucchini, then the tomatoes and finally the sliced scallops. The scallops should reach the top of the pan.

5. Broil for about 5 minutes, remove from pan and drizzle with olive oil to serve.

We serve with an arugula salad topped with locatelli cheese, lemon juice and olive oil. Riondo Prosecco adds a nice sparkle.

The **Italian Side** of **Dan Butler**

*D*an Butler sort of stumbled across Italy.

Butler is one of the two most-famous Delaware-based restaurateurs, and his Piccolina Toscana in Trolley Square—the third incarnation of his Toscana brand—has now gone through one 20-year-lease, and Butler is now working on a second.

In recent years, he has expanded through partnerships to open Deep Blue in Wilmington and twin properties in Chadds Ford—Bistro on the Brandywine and Brandywine Prime Seafood and Chops.

But it's Toscana that introduced Butler, a Delaware native, to Wilmington dining.

"After the CIA (Culinary Institute of America), I got my first job at Tiberio at 19th and K in Washington," he says, referring to the famous eatery that was home away from home for many K Street lobbyists.

That led him to consider opening his own Italian restaurant—"It was what I knew best"—and he finally found a place in Wilmington, after first looking at other cities that he liked.

"I had in mind an upscale, northern Italian restaurant," he recalls, "but I ended up building a restaurant around the space." It was an immediate success, and Butler's career was launched.

As I've said elsewhere, Butler is known for three things—his great food, willingness to talk to reporters about whatever is in the foodie news loop and giving back to the community through his extensive non-profit work.

We talked him into giving us the recipes for his Figaro pizzette and calamari fritti.

PICCOLINA TOSCANA | WILMINGTON

WWW.PICCOLINATOSCANA.COM

Figaro Pizzette

Chef Dan Butler

Serves: 1

INGREDIENTS

1	pizzette dough (see recipe below)
½ cup	grated mozzarella
¼ cup	gorgonzola
4	fresh figs cut into quarters. (If fresh figs aren't available, you can use dry figs. Just put them in a small sauce pot, cover them with water and honey and simmer until softened)
4 slices	pancetta
2 tbsp.	truffle honey (To make truffle honey, simmer 1 cup of honey. Once it has come to a simmer, slowly whisk in 2 tbsp. of truffle oil. Refrigerate and reserve.)
1 cup	olive oil

PREPARATION

1. Preheat oven with pizza stone in it to 500 degrees or as high as it will go.

2. Roll the dough out to a 12-inch disk on a floured work surface with a rolling pin.

3. Brush the dough with olive oil and sprinkle the mozzarella over the dough evenly leaving about a quarter inch of dough uncovered around the edge. Next, spread the gorgonzola in the same manner. Now arrange the pancetta and figs so that they are evenly placed over the cheese.

4. Using a floured pizza peel (spatula), place the dough in the oven. Rotate a quarter turn every 2 or 3 minutes or so to ensure even browning. Once it is crispy and the cheese is sufficiently brown, remove, slice and enjoy.

PIZZETTE DOUGH INGREDIENTS
Makes 4 pizzettes

1 ½ cups	warm water
½ tsp.	active dry yeast
2 tsp.	extra virgin olive oil
2 ½ tsp.	kosher salt
4 cups	high-gluten flour

PREPARATION

1. In the bowl of an electric mixer fitted with the paddle attachment, mix together the yeast and water for about 10 minutes. The mix should be frothy. If it is not, then you need to start over with a pack of fresh yeast.

2. Add the extra virgin olive oil and kosher salt.

3. Add the flour and mix until the dough pulls away from the bowl. The dough should be strong enough that when you stretch it between your hands and hold it to the light, you can see the light shine through without any holes. This is called the window-pane test.

4. Oil a bowl large enough to hold double the dough and place the dough in the bowl topped with a damp towel. Allow this to sit in your refrigerator overnight.

5. Remove the dough from the refrigerator. On a floured work surface, divide into 4 even pieces.

6. Gently roll the 4 pieces into 4 balls and allow to rest covered with a damp towel for an hour until ready to make the pizzette.

CALAMARI FRITTI

CHEF DAN BUTLER

"I had in mind an upscale, northern Italian restaurant," Dan recalls, *"but I ended up building a restaurant around the space."*

Serves: 4

INGREDIENTS

I lb.	calamari (Look or ask for tubes and tentacles. Slice the tubes into ¼ inch rings and cut the tentacle portion in half.)
I	red bell pepper sliced
8	cherry tomatoes cut in half
I tbsp.	garlic powder
I tbsp.	Pimenton
I tbsp.	onion powder
½ tbsp.	ground ginger
2 cups	all-purpose flour
2 cups	stone ground corn meal
I cup	buttermilk
2 tbsp.	chopped chives
salt and pepper to taste	

PREPARATION

1. Preheat a tabletop fryer to 375 degrees.

2. Place the calamari, bell pepper and cherry tomato in a shallow bowl and cover it with the buttermilk.

3. Sift together the flour, corn meal, garlic powder, ginger, onion powder and Pimenton into a separate bowl.

4. With a slotted spoon, remove the calamari mixture from the buttermilk, making sure to drain well of any excess buttermilk, and place it in the flour mixture. Gently toss the calamari in the breading, being sure that it is evenly coated. It has a tendency to bunch together so separating it with your hand may be necessary to fully coat everything. Shake off any residual flour and place in the fryer.

5. Fry for approximately 6 minutes or until golden. Remove the basket from the fryer and allow the oil to drain for 30 seconds.

6. Toss the calamari in a bowl with salt, pepper and the fresh chives.

Farm to Table at **Doe Run**

For Kristian Holbrook and Haesel Charlesworth, farm to table is a way of everyday life.

Both Kristian and Haesel are former professional chefs, and, as the husband-and-wife management team at The Farm at Doe Run northwest of Unionville, she raises large crops of vegetables for sale at market and for the table, and he tends herds of cows, goats and sheep and makes a variety of different-style cheeses from their milk in the farm's ultra-modern milk barn and cheese-processing facility.

"I always believe that the quality of cheese is dependent on the quality of care that you give your animals," he says, as he rubs the ear of a goat while a nearby cow eyes him.

Doe Run—the old Thouron estate—is an idyllic setting for the couple to farm and to raise their young daughter, Violette.

There are acres of meadows and fields for the animals to graze and places for cats to roam and chickens to wander free-range. Fox hunters ride to the hounds nearby. The busy couple lives in an often renovated and added-to 18th Century farmhouse that has marvelous views of the valley.

They had previously worked in a similar capacity at the showplace Blackberry Farm in East Tennessee and, while they find things equally hectic here, it is somewhat more quiet without the food tourists in the upper reaches of the Brandywine Valley.

Being invited to have a late-afternoon, weekend meal with Haesel and Kristian is a treat. "We have different ways of cooking," Haesel says, as she explains that the blue-colored polenta she has made is molded, while Kristian prefers to make polenta looser and free-form. "The polenta is from our corn," she says, an heirloom variety

called Bloody Butcher that she grinds into meal herself. She is serving it with Little Gem romaine and asparagus—a gorgeous combination of flavors and textures.

Kristian, meanwhile, is grilling a boned leg of lamb—some tied, some in chunks—over a wood fire. "He's better at meats than I am," Haesel says, and indeed he "knows" when it's almost done without a thermometer or slicing off a piece. A few minutes before the meat is ready, he starts making spinach tarts. "We always use suet for taste and texture," he says. "Is it OK if we use it in the recipe for the book?" We assure him it is. "It's a non-traditional tart without a tart pan," he explains, as his hands work quickly to make four rounded pieces of dough before adding creamed spinach in the middle of each and then curling up the edges. It goes into the hot oven for a quick bake.

When it all comes together, Ella and I add to the meal a treat we have brought—six bottles of hand-made, fruit-based wines from our neighbor, David Schlueter. Currant wine, elderberry wine, plum wine (from 2005), spiced apple wine and two kinds of cherry wine. They are all superb.

Then a large truck comes up the driveway full of hay just recently baled in an adjacent field on the farm, and Kristian has to go off to unload the bales into the loft of the milk barn. It is a hot day and the fields are verdant, but the cows, and sheep and goats will appreciate the hay come winter.

Spinach and Sultana Tarts

RECIPE

Kristian Holbrook

Serves: 4-6

INGREDIENTS FOR TART DOUGH

14 oz.	self-rising flour
½ tsp.	salt
7 oz.	shredded beef suet, or vegetarian shortening
1 ¼ cup	cold water

INGREDIENTS FOR SPINACH FILLING

1	large red onion, thinly sliced
¼	stick of butter or olive oil
3 lbs.	fresh spinach, preferably with roots attached, chopped roughly
1 cup	sultanas
½	fresh whole nutmeg, grated
½ cup	cream, if desired
1	lemon's worth of lemon's zest
salt to taste	

PREPARATION

1. Heat a large pan over medium heat and add butter or oil, then onion and cook until it is slowly, thoroughly browned. Take your time, as this step is important to the quality of the finished tart.

2. Add sultanas and stir. Add spinach and increase heat slightly. Cook until spinach is wilted. Drain excess spinach juice.

3. Press spinach in a strainer to extract any remaining water. Return spinach to pan and add cream. Season to taste with nutmeg, lemon zest (not juice) and salt. Allow filling to cool slightly.

4. Next, combine dough ingredients to make free-form tart shells 4-6 inches in diameter or use tart pans to make individual tart bases.

5. Add filling to uncooked shells, and, if free-form, fold in edges. Bake at 375 degrees until slightly browned.

POLENTA WITH ASPARAGUS AND LETTUCE

HAESEL CHARLESWORTH

"I like to make polenta in the spring. I have listed the water to cornmeal ratio at 3:1 for a firm, sliceable polenta that keeps its shape. The coarser the corn grind, the longer the cooking time."

Serves: 4

INGREDIENTS

6 cups	water
I tsp.	salt
2 cups	finely ground cornmeal
I	white onion
I	bunch asparagus
3	small heads of bib, mini romaine or Boston lettuce

olive oil
Doe Run aged gouda for shaving

PREPARATION

1.   Preheat oven to 350 degrees.

2.   Boil 6 cups water and turn heat off. Dissolve salt into water, then add cornmeal and whisk together. Cornmeal should thicken to the consistency of porridge.

3.   Pour the cornmeal into a square, greased bread pan, cover with foil and set in a shallow pan of hot water. Place into oven and bake 30 minutes.

4.   Meanwhile, thinly slice the onion and asparagus. Toss with olive oil, salt and pepper and distribute thinly on a sheet pan.

5.   When your polenta is out of the oven, turn up the heat to 450 degrees and pop in the asparagus and onions.

6.   Cut bib lettuce in half. Toss with olive oil and salt, put cut side down on sheet pans and roast along with the asparagus—though they will require less time.

7.   Remove vegetables from oven when the outer surface is quite crisp and browned.

8.   Cool your polenta to just about room temperature, slice, and alternate on individual plates with layers of roasted lettuce and asparagus/onion.

9.   Top with some shaved cheese such as ricotta salata or, if you can get ours at Doe Run—well, that's better—Seven Sisters aged gouda.

THE SUMMER

THE LIGHTNESS OF BEING

Music floats out through the screen of the open window, wraps itself around the rocking chairs that are motionless on the shaded porch, then drifts like the morning mist down across the greenness of the backyard and disappears among the oaks, the beeches and the poplars of the woods. The quiet pools in the stream are without ripples.

No matter how busy we think we are, there reaches those delicious summer moments on the warm sand at the beach, in a deck chair reading, in the bedroom as the sun slowly wakes us up that time simply slows down to a shuffle. Have we fallen asleep, or is time itself dreaming?

Yet summer is our time to break the routine by spending the afternoon with a drink by the pool and taking a leisurely walk around the block.

And is there any one season that has so totally dedicated itself to our relaxation? Of course, we still work, we play hard, we sweat.

Yet summer is our time to break the routine, to go cross-country on family vacations, sneak out of the office early on Fridays to head for the mountains or the beach, spend the afternoon with a drink by the pool, smoke a cigar and leisurely walk around the block after dinner.

And it's a great time to catch up with the wealth of local museums and gardens. For foodies, try to get tickets to the annual Stroud Water Research Center's outdoor sustainable feast, with farm-to-table food prepared under the auspices of Aimee Olexy and her Talula's Table restaurant in Kennett Square.

Summer, for those old enough to understand the analogy, is the time when our hectic 45 rpm lives slow down to a 33⅓ pace.

Stillabowers: Brandywiners at the Beach

No matter how beautiful our summers along the Brandywine, most everyone wants to get away for at least one week in the mountains (Poconos), on the shore (Jersey) or at the beach (Delaware).

We have known Mike and Jennifer Stillabowers for a long time—in wine groups, cooking groups, parties and dinners, even vacationing together in Bordeaux, California, Peru, and, last spring, Santa Fe. Jennifer is a dyed-in-the-linen foodie foodie, both in terms of searching out best restaurants while traveling and in her love of cooking. As Michael is a cardiologist, we all ask him about the dangers of our over-indulging, even if we do consume a lot of antioxidants in red wine.

A few years ago, the Stillabowers bought a beautiful beach house on one of the canals that make South Bethany Beach the Venice of Delaware, but it wasn't long before Jennifer was giving it a complete makeover, making it even lovelier than it was before. Chez Stillabowers South is a beautiful place to be invited for a summer weekend. (Although it may be less prestigious than Chez Stillabowers North, where their next door neighbor happens to be Vice President Biden.)

The weekend might start with some shopping Friday afternoon, dinner out in Rehoboth Beach on Friday night, a walk and a Bloody Mary breakfast on Saturday, followed by a shopping and gallery hopping trip to a nearby small town, such as Snow Hill or Berlin, where we can lunch on the porch of the Atlantic Hotel. Then a brief afternoon nap before having hors d'oeuvres on board the Stillabowers' boat as we cruise through the canals (No Wakes, Please!) into one of the bays before returning back to the house for one of Jennifer's wonderful dinners and lots of wine.

This evening, dinner is fat crab cakes in a pretty puddle of green basil dressing and a medley of sweet corn and juicy tomatoes. For dessert, Jennifer brings out locally made blueberry pie with freshly made whipped cream.

We may have to sleep in on Sunday.

RECIPE

Roasted Eggplant Spread (Caponata)

Jennifer Stillabower

"I usually serve with feta, dolmades and hummus dip. The original recipe is from Ina Garten."

Serves: 8

INGREDIENTS

1	medium eggplant, peeled
2	red peppers, peeled
1	red onion, peeled
2	cloves garlic, minced
3 tbsp.	olive oil
1 tsp.	kosher salt
½ tsp.	black pepper
1 tbsp.	tomato paste

PREPARATION

1. Cut the vegetables into one-inch cubes and toss them in a large bowl with olive oil, salt and pepper.

2. Spread them on a foil-lined baking sheet that has been sprayed with Pam. In an oven pre-heated to 400 degrees, roast them for 45 minutes or until the vegetables are soft and lightly browned, tossing once during the baking.

3. Cool slightly, then place the vegetables in a processor. Add tomato paste and chop by pulsing 3 or 4 times to blend. Taste for salt and pepper. (May be made a day or two ahead.)

4. Serve with pita chips or any Mediterranean-style chip.

Crab Cakes with Basil Dressing and Marinated Tomatoes and Corn

Jennifer Stillabower

"This recipe is inspired by one from Tyler Florence."

Serves: 4-6

INGREDIENTS FOR CRAB CAKES

2 lbs.	jumbo lump crabmeat
1 ½ cups	bread crumbs made from 4-5 slices of white bread, crusts removed and processed in processor.
2-3 tbsp.	mayonnaise (can add a little more if needed)
2	egg whites, lightly whisked
½	lemon, juiced
1 tsp.	Old Bay seasoning or to taste

sprinkle of cayenne to taste (optional)
sea salt and freshly ground pepper

PREPARATION FOR CRAB CAKES

1. Mix all ingredients until just blended, shape into about 8-10 cakes, place on parchment lined baking sheet and cover loosely.

2. Chill in refrigerator several hours to set.

3. Saute the crab cakes in 3 tbsp. of olive oil in a large non-stick sauté pan for 4 minutes per side until brown and crisp.

continued on page 78

RECIPE

Crab Cakes with Basil Dressing and Marinated Tomatoes and Corn...continued from page 77

INGREDIENTS FOR DRESSING

½ cup	buttermilk
½ cup	mayonnaise
½ cup	sour cream
½ cup	fresh basil leaves (can use more if you like)
2 tbsp.	olive oil
few drops of lemon juice	
sea salt to taste	

PREPARATION FOR DRESSING

Combine in a blender and puree until smooth. Note: This should be served at room temperature, so set out of refrigerator for at least 15 minutes before serving.

INGREDIENTS FOR MARINATED CORN AND TOMATOES

4 ears	corn, unshucked
2	ripe tomatoes, cut into wedges
1	pint container of grape tomatoes, cut in half
1 tbsp.	Old Bay seasoning
2 tbsp.	lemon juice
¼ cup	olive oil
1 tbsp.	tiny basil leaves and some additional basil chiffonade
sea salt and pepper to taste	

PREPARATION FOR MARINATED CORN AND TOMATOES

1. Roast corn on oven racks at 350 degrees for 30 minutes, until husks are brownish. (The corn will steam in the jackets.)

2. When cool enough to handle, husk the corn and slice the kernels into a mixing bowl.

3. Toss in the tomatoes, seasonings and oil. Refrigerate. (This can be done up to an hour in advance.)

ASSEMBLY

Spoon some dressing on each plate and place one or two crab cakes in the center. Sprinkle with tomato-corn mixture and serve immediately.

All Is Sweet at **Capers & Lemons**

After opening Eclipse Bistro on Union Street along Wilmington's restaurant row and then launching Dome—later retro-fitted as Redfire Grill—in suburban Hockessin, Carl Georigi and the Platinum Dining Group took a gamble and placed its third entry, Capers & Lemons, a large Italian restaurant, in the no-man's land between city and country.

True, a few large office buildings are located nearby along Centre Road, but few local restaurants have been able to survive on a lunch-time business alone, especially these days when corporate types no longer drink like "Mad Men."

However, Capers & Lemons has flourished, sporting a large bar that is generally full-up after work, except during the summer months when people flock to the beach, shore and mountains for vacations and weekends.

There is always a large booking of tables at dinner as well as lunch, and Georigi has also installed a market in a large room just off the entry lobby stocked with basic cooking ingredients and canned produce for the home cooks to take with them.

But, as with the other restaurants in the group, Capers & Lemons has flourished primarily because of its good food—an excellent menu well-executed. Chef Mike O'Hare can take a deep bow.

Next, Newark will go "Platinum" when the group's fourth restaurant—Taverna—opens in the fall of 2012.

CAPERS & LEMONS | WILMINGTON
302.256.0524

RECIPE

Sweet Corn Agnolotti

Chef Mike O'Hare

"Prepared pasta sheets are available at larger supermarkets and also Italian markets."

Serves: 4-6

INGREDIENTS

6 ears	sweet corn
1 tbsp.	mascarpone cheese
1 tbsp.	butter
¾ cup	heavy cream
pinch	fresh tarragon
salt and pepper to taste	
pasta sheets to make 24-30 6-in circles	

PREPARATION

1. On a box grater, grate corn on the cob over a large bowl and set aside.

2. Over medium heat reduce heavy cream by half, add grated corn and its liquid crema.

3. Cook until mixture begins to get dry. Add mascarpone, tarragon, butter, salt and pepper. Combine everything with a spoon and place in refrigerator to chill.

4. Cut out three-circles from your pasta sheets. Place 1 tbsp. of corn filling in center of the circle. Brush half of the circle with an egg wash, fold over and press edge firmly. Repeat.

5. Place each finished agnolotti on a sheet pan and refrigerate (freeze if you are going to cook them the next day).

RECIPE

INGREDIENTS FOR CORN SAUCE

1 cup	sweet corn
1 cup	tomato, chopped
¼ cup	extra virgin olive oil
¼ cup	white wine
¼ cup	vegetable stock
¼ cup	shallot, chopped
1 tbsp.	basil
4 tbsp.	butter
salt and pepper to taste	

PREPARATION FOR CORN SAUCE

1. Heat olive oil in saucepan over medium heat. Add shallots and saute lightly for 1 minute. Add sweet corn and tomato and cook for 2 minutes. Add white wine and cook an additional 2 minutes then add vegetable stock. Bring to a boil, lower heat, add basil and butter.

2. Bring a large pot of salted water to a boil and cook agnolotti for 2 minutes (fresh) or 4 minutes (frozen).

3. Place agnolotti in pan with sauce, coat evenly and plate. Top with sauce and corn. Garnish with fresh basil.

RECIPE

Summer Ratatouille

Chef Mike O'Hare

Serves: 8 as a side dish

INGREDIENTS

1	eggplant, cubed
1	zucchini, cubed
1	yellow squash, cubed
½	red bell pepper, diced
1	Spanish onion, finely diced
2	28 oz. cans crushed tomatoes
2	cloves garlic, crushed
¼ cup	grated parmesan cheese
¼ cup	basil, chopped
¼ cup	parsley, chopped
1 tbsp.	thyme, chopped
1 tbsp.	salt
1 tsp.	pepper
½ cup	extra virgin olive oil
1 cup	red wine vinegar
½ cup	sugar

PREPARATION

 RECIPE

1. Pour vinegar into a saucepan over high heat and bring to a boil. Add sugar and turn down heat to medium. Reduce to half and set aside.

2. Pour ¼ cup olive oil in large pan over medium heat. Add onions, pepper, garlic, salt, pepper, thyme. Cook until onions are transparent.

3. Add eggplant and cook 5 more minutes, stirring occasionally. Add squash and tomatoes and bring to a boil. Reduce heat and simmer 15 minutes.

4. Add basil, parsley, parmesan and remaining olive oil. Cook for 5 more minutes, remove pan from heat and stir in red wine vinegar reductions.

5. Serve as side dish.

6. Turn out on to lightly floured work surface and cut in to two pieces. Knead each to form a pleasing loaf shape. Place each in a pan, seam side down, pinching seams together.

7. Slash (not cut down in to) top surface with knife in parallel diagonals or diagonal crisscross pattern to allow bread to vent while baking. Brush with egg white wash, sprinkle with cracked sea salt if desired.

8. Let rise until doubled, then place in pre-heated oven at 425 degrees for 10 minutes. Open door to check. Reduce heat to 375 degrees for 20-30 minutes until pleasingly golden brown on top.

9. Remove from pans when done, let sit on side till cool.

Cardile Mushrooms: The Next Generation

Fresh mushrooms are the economic lifeblood of much of the Brandywine region, supplying the delicacy to most of the eastern United States in refrigerated trucks on an overnight basis—picked one day here and on grocery shelves the next day there.

The towns of Kennett Square, Avondale and Toughkennamon are the heart of a region, with low, squat mushroom barns dotting the landscape while large trucks haul in hay—which long ago replaced horse manure as the fertile processed soil—that is harvested both from local meadows and from as far away as the plains of Canada.

Many of these mushroom businesses are owned by families who forebears came here from Italy, where mushrooms are a national passion. Through the years, their production has expanded from the white button to the brown button (criminis) to the big button (portobello or portabella) to exotics like shitakes and inokis.

Such is the story of brothers Matt and Charles Cardile. Their grandfather, Salvatore, emigrated from Sicily in the 1920s, and the family has been growing mushrooms ever since. "We're the next generation," Matt says, outside the Cardile complex of mushroom barns beside a large field used for turning hay into steaming—and smelly—mountains of mushroom compost on a hillside just outside of Avondale.

"Our biggest customer is Costco," Charles says. So even if you buy some of your produce at this large-box chain, your mushrooms are still picked locally.

CARDILE MUSHROOMS
AVONDALE

RECIPE

Mushroom Salad with Prosciutto and Sweet Balsamic Vinaigrette

Cardile Mushrooms

Serves: 6

INGREDIENTS

2 cups	arugula, chopped or torn
I cup	radicchio, chopped or torn
I cup	baby spinach
2	portobellos, cut into ¼ inch slices
I cup	sliced gourmet mushrooms
⅓ lb.	prosciutto, thinly sliced
2 tbsp.	dried cherries
¼ lb.	cheese, thinly shaved

INGREDIENTS FOR THE SWEET BALSAMIC VINAIGRETTE

¾ cup	balsamic vinegar
¼ cup	red wine vinegar
3 tbsp.	extra virgin olive oil
3 tbsp.	vegetable oil
2 tbsp.	sun-dried tomato puree
¼ tsp.	garlic, chopped
¼ tbsp.	fresh basil, chopped

PREPARATION

1. Combine the greens and mushrooms in a salad bowl.

2. Make the vinaigrette by whisking together everything but the oils, then slowly drizzle in the oils while whisking to emulsified.

3. Pour the vinaigrette over the salad and top with cherries, prosciutto and the cheese shavings.

Portoburgers

Cardile Mushrooms

Serves: 4

INGREDIENTS

4	large Portobello caps
½ cup	extra-virgin olive oil
¼ cup	fresh herbs, chopped
4	smoked mozzarella slices
4	lettuce slices
4	small tomato slices
4	buns

PREPARATION

1. Coat the mushroom caps with oil and herbs.

2. Grill caps about 4 minutes per side.

3. Just before removing from grill, put a slice of cheese on each cap to melt.

4. Assemble the burgers.

Crab Feast **at Fair Hill**

Chefs Phil Pyle and Brian Shaw prepare elegant meals at Fair Hill Inn in nearby Maryland, but they love nothing more than having a down-and-dirty crab feast on a summer's evening. As Phil reminds me whenever I say "clam bakes," that's what the New England folks do. (OK, truth be told, Ella and I have a family place on Martha's Vineyard.)

Phil's family came to the Brandywine region it seems even before William Penn (notice how many local roads have "Pyle" in the name and how many paintings in the Brandywine River Museum were done by a Pyle), while Brian comes from the lower Chesapeake, where they do all the same things Phil's people do—only differently. On slow days, the two probably worry about what they will line their crab feasts table with when all newspapers go digital.

Anyway, we asked Phil and Brian, who think that recipes are like road maps for people who don't have mental built-in GPS cooking systems, to lay out some ground rules for throwing our own crab feasts.

First, buy your beer, newspapers and Old Bay. Then read on.

FAIR HILL INN
FAIR HILL, MARYLAND

How to Hold Your Own Crab Feast

Chefs Phil Pyle and Brian Shaw

1.   Identify those guests who are "new" to crabs. Pair them at the table with an expert who can show them how the crab is opened and consumed. Tell them not to eat the lungs and that when you use a hammer to open the claws, hit the side of the claw that is the lightest in color. This is the side that has the thinnest shell and therefore easiest to crack.

2.   Crab feasts are just that—a feast of "crabs"—so use the correct terminology. No self-respecting mid-Atlantic person would refer to crabs as "hard shells" or blue crabs – it's implied. If you want to look like a local, talk like one.

3.   Have non-seafood offerings for those guests who do not eat crab due to allergies, for kids or for those who fear the crab.

4.   Notwithstanding the above, make sure all children attempt to eat at least one crab. We can't keep tradition going if the younger generations eat only mac and cheese.

5.   Have your crab feast outdoors. If you hold it indoors, you will smell old seafood for the next three weeks.

continued on page 94

RECIPE

Crab Feast...continued from page 92

6.   Try to seat everyone at one long table, Italian-style. It's much more fun, and when you take a picture, it will look very "Martha Stewart-like" and possibly worth framing.

7.   Start saving newspapers at least two weeks before the feast. They are the tablecloth. No experienced crab feast expert would serve these beautiful creatures on anything but the finest newsprint.

8.   Place paper towel rolls every four feet on the table for proper clean-up. If you are so inclined, place finger bowls with quartered lemons for guests to clean up after eating, although this is not very traditional. Locals will simply pour beer on their hands to rinse and dry off with paper towels.

9.   Beer—have plenty of it and make damn sure it is cold. Keep ice chests of beer within easy walking (stumbling) distance from the table. Stick with "pils," "helles" or other light styles. Avoid imperial IPA's, stouts (yuck!) or porters (double yuck). Remember, you need to cook crabs in that beer, so buy enough for the pot and for everyone else.

10.   To appease those who do not drink beer with their crabs (this is almost sacrilege), make sure you have lots of ice tea. If you have wine drinkers, make sure you have lots of rosé—perhaps the most under-appreciated wine in the world. It goes great with crab. But remember—rosé has alcohol, and when you are not walking straight due to over-consumption, cleaning up takes on a whole new twist.

11.   When you order your crabs, make sure you order live crabs. Always steam them yourself (in beer, water and Old Bay and salt). When you buy live, you can identify those crabs that are dead, and those dead guys need to be thrown away. Eating a crab that was dead before it was cooked is a sure way to find yourself praying to the porcelain god.)

12.   Have big trashcans with extra-strong liners for clean-up, but make sure these trashcans are a fair distance away from the table because they attract flies. Secure the lid and the can so it will not topple. Dogs and other critters love crabs.

13.   Bon appetit.

Va La Vineyards: Wine, Food and Music

Over the past dozen years, farm wineries have been popping up over the region like dandelions in a spring pasture. At present, there are at least a dozen. A few years ago, who would have thought that Kennett Square, Avondale, Chadds Ford, West Grove or Landenberg would be "wine towns' with one, maybe two, vineyard-and-winery estates within their zip codes?

Although bustling and cozy in the winter, these wineries blossom in the summer, as everyone moves outside. Food vendors—like the pizza man and the barbecue guy—are summoned, and the afternoons and evenings come alive with the sounds of jazz, rock and country served up by local bands. Local wine, local food, local music!

One of our favorite destinations is the small in size but high in quality Va La Vineyards located on a hillside along Route 41 just southwest of Avondale. For the last dozen years, Anthony Vietri has been making great northern Italian style reds, whites and rosatos, while his wife Karen and the family run the tasting room. Anthony and Karen are the fourth generation to farm here, and daughter Sofia is the fifth.

Keyboardist Glenn E. Williams is almost like family, having played upstairs in the Galleria since the winery opened. During the summer, he shifts from solo to trio, as his jazz group entertains Va La patrons who take to lawn chairs and picnic blankets while they drink Anthony's wine and order pies from the pizza vendor or enjoy their own picnics.

Too bad they can't savor Anthony's cooking. We have on a few occasions, and, while we wouldn't want him to ever abandon his winemaking, he could have a good following as a farm-to-table chef.

VA LA VINEYARDS

AVONDALE, PENNSYLVANIA

COUNTRY BRINED AND ROASTED RABBIT

ANTHONY VIETRI

Serves: 2

INGREDIENTS

1	whole rabbit
¼ cup	extra virgin olive oil
½ tsp.	kosher salt
	fine black pepper
	fresh rosemary, about 4 three-inch branches diced into small pieces. (Do not attempt to substitute dry rosemary)
4 cloves	garlic, peeled and crushed
1	medium-sized onion, quartered
1 cup	fine dry rosato, dry rose or rabato wine. (Va la Silk works well)
1	2 gallon-size freezer bag or a covered roasting pan

PREPARATION

1. 12 to 24 hours before, clean and then chop rabbit into 6 to 8 sections. Place sections into a two-gallon freezer bag (or a covered roasting pan). Add the other ingredients to the rabbit. Seal and place in fridge overnight.

2. Remove rabbit from container and place in a roasting pan. Add to the roasting pan all the solid contents from the marinade bag while holding back the liquid. Once this is completed, now add enough liquid from the marinade bag to the roasting pan to a height of about ¼ inch in the pan. Retain the remainder of the liquid to be slowly added back to the pan as the rabbit cooks.

3. Cover and place pan in oven at temperature of 400 degrees.

4. As the rabbit cooks, add back small amounts of the brine marinade. You will want to use all of the marinade by approximately 20 minutes cooking time.

5. At about 25-30 minutes cooking time, remove cover to allow marinade to cook down, and the rabbit to brown. Cooking time will be about 35-45 minutes depending on oven and pan, or until flesh is white to the bone but not dry.

6. Serve with a rosato wine, such as Va La Silk.

RECIPE

OYSTER MUSHROOM AND DANDELION PASTA

ANTHONY VIETRI

Serves: 6

INGREDIENTS

5	large bunches of freshly picked dandelions. (Try to select those from a shaded location for best flavors).
2 lbs.	fresh Avondale oyster mushrooms
2 cups	white wine, preferably La Prima Donna
4 cloves	garlic
	extra virgin olive oil
½ to 1 lb.	spaghetti # 4, 6, or 8
¼ stick	butter
	kosher salt and fine black pepper
	fresh shaved or grated Pecorino Romano

continued on page 102

RECIPE

Oyster Mushroom and Dandelion Pasta...continued from page 100

PREPARATION

I.   Thoroughly clean and then chop fresh dandelion into small sections. Set aside to drain.

2.   Clean and remove stumps from oyster mushrooms. Coarsely chop into long, wide sections.

3.   Bring one pasta pot of water to boil. Add about I tsp. kosher salt—salt the water so that it tastes of salt, but is not "salty."

4.   Lightly oil a large but deep-sided skillet. Using medium flame, sauté garlic until white with amber edges. Immediately add oyster mushrooms to the pan. At about 2 minutes, the mushrooms should begin to release liquid. Add about 2 cups of La Prima Donna white wine, plus ¼ stick of butter. Add salt and pepper to the sauce to taste. Simmer about 10 minutes.

5.   At this point, add pasta to the boiling pot while mushrooms continue to simmer. At about the 5-minute point, remove partially cooked pasta and drain briefly. Then quickly add pasta to the skillet with the mushrooms.

6.   Finish cooking the pasta in the sauce for about 3 to 5 more minutes, tasting regularly to make sure that you remove the pasta from the fire when it is lightly al dente.

7.   At al dente, remove the pasta to a large bowl. Immediately add the freshly cut dandelions to the steaming pasta, and toss lightly. Place the pasta in plates and shave or grate pecorino directly and copiously onto the warm bed of pasta.

8.   Serve with a chilled Va La Prima Donna or similar white wine.

THE AUTUMN

MORNING CHILL, FALLING LEAVES

You start seeing the signs in August. The weather is still blazingly hot when the narrow leaves of the walnut trees start turning a yellow-green and float down to earth. At the edge of the woods, weeds start to die back and you can see a little further into the forest. You notice the woolly worms crawling across the back roads when you go for a walk. The last of the blackberries have shriveled.

An eternal alarm clock signals. Even though you haven't been in a classroom for ages, and kids today have smart phones, you want to buy yellow No. 2 pencils and a plastic sharpener. You start thinking about where your rake is, how you really want to smell yellow mums, and you notice the skins on those delightful tomatoes you've grown in the back yard start to toughen a bit. It soon will be time for fresh local apples, you think.

The weather is blazingly hot when the narrow leaves of the walnut trees start turning a yellow-green and float down to earth.

*B*efore you know it, you're into September and October. Yellow school buses match the golden leaves that brightly filter the sun, which all of a sudden is farther south in the sky than you remember it. What do I need to bring in before the first frost? How much Halloween candy will I need? The lawn mower gives way to the leaf blower.

Then it's November. Thanksgiving is coming soon. Turkey? Rabbit? Pheasant? Or a butterflied leg of lamb? You drink some hard cider while thinking it over. And just when you think the color show is over, there is a blaze of red to join the yellows.

Then Thanksgiving is gone. Woolens have been brought out. There are a few warm days still left to fool us, but we know another glorious party is over. Time for a final cleanup, to put things away and to move a stack of firewood to the back porch.

Harvesting Grapes with the Manguses

*I*n the Brandywine region, grape harvest usually begin in August, long before most leaves turn red and yellow and before the fodder is in the barns

Tony and Karen Mangus have been growing grapes to sell to regional wineries for a decade, and today their Historic Hopewell Vineyard near Oxford has grown to xxx acres of grapes, most, though not all of them French- and Italian-based varieties—Merlot, Cabernet France, Pinot Gris, Sauvignon Blanc.

As both have full-time jobs—Tony is an international airline pilot, and Karen is a marketing executive—most of their hands-on farming is done evenings and weekends. That necessitates a full-time vineyard manager, and, at harvest, dozens of friends and families of both the manager's and the Manguses.

Much of the exacting day-to-day work in commercial vineyards, such as the Manguses' and at the dozen or so local wineries who grow part of their own grapes is done by local families of Mexican heritage, so Karen's harvest meals are combinations of her own heritage (German), Tony's (Greek) and the manager's (Mexican).

Of course, they are the force that drives grape-growing and the Brandywine area wineries who have grown in number and in quality the last 10 years. Currently, there are 8—all open the visitors:

- Va La (Avondale)
- Chaddsford (Chaddsford)
- Paradocx (Landenberg)
- Kreutz Creek (West Grove)
- Galer Estate (Longwood)
- Stargazers (Coatesville)
- Penns Woods (tasting room near Route 202)
- Patone (Landenberg)

HISTORIC HOPEWELL VINEYARDS | OXFORD
WWW.HISTORICHOPEWELLVINEYARDS.COM

RECIPE

Harvest Chorizo and Potatoes

KAREN MANGUS

Serves: Hungry crew of grape harvesters

INGREDIENTS

2	24 oz. bags of frozen potatoes with onions and peppers
2-3 lbs.	fresh (unsmoked) chorizo or andouille sausage links
salt and pepper	

PREPARATION

1. The night before harvest, place potatoes in colander, allowing them to defrost for several hours.

2. Prior to going to bed (assuming that you can sleep as the upcoming harvest is very exciting), line several flat baking sheets with clean cotton towels or multiple layers of paper towels.

3. Spread potatoes with onions and peppers in a single layer on baking sheets to allow moisture to be removed from the potatoes. Cover with another cotton towel or layers of paper towels to assure they absorb all the moisture.

4. Store overnight in a dry, clean environment, such as an unheated oven.

5. Harvest Day—remove fresh sausage from casings and place in a Dutch oven or large pot and fully cook until lightly crispy.

6. Remove from pan using slotted spoon and place on plate covered with paper towels to remove excess grease. Reserve 6 tbsp. of remaining oil in Dutch oven.

7. Two hours before serving, reheat pan with remaining oil, add thawed/dried potatoes with onions and peppers and cook in oil until coated and warm. Blend in chorizo, warm and serve.

CRISPY SESAME ASPARAGUS BUNDLES

Karen Mangus

Serves: 6

INGREDIENTS

1 lb.	Small-tipped fresh asparagus
10 sheets	9" x 14" phyllo dough
2 sticks	melted butter
2 tbsp.	sesame oil
2 tbsp.	toasted sesame seeds
salt and white pepper to taste	

PREPARATION

1. Preheat oven to 350 degrees.

2. Wash asparagus and trim to uniform length, keeping tips in the same direction. Let dry, then coat asparagus with sesame oil. Salt and pepper. Set aside.

3. Spread one phyllo sheet out on a flat, buttered surface. Brush top of sheet with a generous amount of butter. Layer and butter another sheet, continuing until all 10 sheets are assembled.

4. Quickly cut the 9" by 14" phyllo into 6, 3" by 7" pieces. Gather asparagus into 6 even-size bundles and wrap each with 3" by 7" phyllo strips.

5. Place each bundle on a buttered baking sheet, buttering each bundle one more time. Sprinkle with seeds.

6. Bake in preheated oven until golden brown. Serve immediately using a spatula to remove the bundles.

A Different Open House in Hockessin

The dream of William & Merry—Bill Hoffman and Merry Catanuto—was not that much different from that of other young people who fell in love in someone else's kitchen.

Both were formally trained as chefs—Merry in California and Bill in Pennsylvania—and both have worked in a number of restaurants since their graduation from culinary school. As fate would have it, they met working in one in Delaware in 2000. Together, they found their dream house—a 90-year-old farm house in the middle of Hockessin, now a thriving crossroads town, and in 2011 opened it to the public as their dream restaurant, the House of William & Merry.

Actually, it is the House of William & Merry & Nicky, their 9-year-old son, for the three of them live upstairs of the renovated house.

Their house is open and bright, with a gleaming open kitchen opposite the entry-area bar along with airy seating areas upstairs and down.

Although the atmosphere in that of an upscale bistro, the food is anything but. Bill, who runs the kitchen and crafts the seasonal menus, is a perfectionist at detail, and his creations are a treat to the eye as well as the palate. If you want a challenging recipe to replicate in your own kitchen, you have only to turn the page.

The House of William & Merry, as the poets of another generation sang, "is a mighty, mighty fine house."

THE HOUSE OF WILLIAM & MERRY | HOCKESSIN

WWW.WILLIAMANDMERRY.COM

RECIPE

CAKE OF AWESOMENESS

CHEF MERRY CATANUTO

Serves: 6

CAKE INGREDIENTS—yields 2 half-sheets or 2 9" rounds

14 oz.	egg whites	15 oz.	sugar
7 ½ oz.	sugar	8 ½ oz.	cake flour
8	egg yolks	7 oz.	cocoa powder
9 oz.	vegetable oil	1 ½ tsp.	baking powder
8 ½ oz.	water	1 ½ tsp.	baking soda

PREPARATION OF CAKE

1.   Beat egg whites until foamy. Slowly add 5 oz. sugar and beat on high until medium peaks form and set aside.

2.   Combine egg yolks, oil, water and 10 oz. sugar in mixing bowl and whisk on low until combined.

3.   In a separate bowl combine cake flour, cocoa powder, baking soda and baking powder.

4.   Add flour mixture to egg yolk mixture and whisk on low for 30 seconds. Turn speed up to medium and whisk for one minute.

5.   Fold egg whites into the chocolate mixture until well combined.

6.   Spread onto 2 half-sheet pans lined with parchment paper or 2 9" rounds that have been greased and flowered.

7.   Bake at 350 degrees until the center of the cake does not jiggle when touched. Allow cakes to cool

PEANUT BUTTER MOUSSE INGREDIENTS

½ cup	creamy peanut butter	1 tbsp.	sugar
¼ cup	packed light brown sugar	1 tsp.	vanilla extract
1 cup	heavy whipping cream	**pinch of salt**	

PREPARATION OF PEANUT BUTTER MOUSSE

1.   Whip ½ cup heavy cream until stiff peaks form and set aside.

2.   Combine peanut butter, brown sugar, salt, ½ cup heavy cream, sugar, and vanilla in a mixing bowl. Whisk on medium speed for 3 minutes.

3.   Fold whipped cream into peanut butter mixture until combined.

INGREDIENTS FOR CHOCOLATE GANACHE

8 oz.   semi-sweet chocolate
8 oz.   heavy whipping cream

PREPARATION OF CHOCOLATE GANACHE

1. Finely chop chocolate and place into a large mixing bowl.

2. Heat heavy cream in saucepan until it just begins to boil. Add cream to chocolate and let sit for 1 minute.

3. With a rubber spatula gently stir mixture until all cream is incorporated and all the chocolate has melted.

INGREDIENTS FOR CARAMEL

7 oz.   sugar
10 ½ oz. heavy whipping cream
4 oz.   light corn syrup
1 oz.   milk chocolate, finely chopped
2 ½ oz.   unsalted butter softened

PREPARATION OF CARAMEL

1. In a large saucepot cook sugar on medium heat until it becomes the color of peanut butter.

2. In another saucepot heat the cream and corn syrup until hot but not boiling.

3. Once the sugar is cooked, slowly add the cream mixture (caution: it may splash and pop). Cook on medium heat whisking often until all sugar is melted. Pour into a bowl and allow to cool for 30 minutes.

4. Once cooled, add the chocolate and butter. Blend until smooth.

PEANUT BRITTLE INGREDIENTS

3 ½ oz.	sugar	**¼ tsp.**	baking soda
1 oz.	butter	**¼ tbsp.**	salt
1 oz.	light corn syrup	**3 oz.**	finely chopped salted peanuts
¾ oz.	water		

PREPARATION OF PEANUT BRITTLE

1. Cook sugar, butter, corn syrup and water in saucepot over medium heat until the color of peanut butter.

2. Combine baking soda, salt and peanuts. Add nut mixture to sugar mixture and stir with a rubber spatula.

3. Pour out onto a Silpat non-stick baking sheet and cover with another Silpat sheet. Roll prattle very thin and allow to cool.

4. Once cooled smash brittle up very fine.   *continued on page 116*

RECIPE

Cake of Awesomeness...continued from page 115

INGREDIENTS FOR CHOCOLATE TUILE

8 oz.   milk chocolate candy melts

PREPARATION OF CHOCOLATE TUILE

1.   Melt chocolate in microwave for 10 seconds at a time until completely melted, stirring after each heating.

2.   Once the chocolate has melted drizzle chocolate with a fork onto parchment paper in a criss-crossed pattern.

3.   Allow to cool then break into pieces.

INGREDIENTS FOR ESPRESSO FOAM

4 shots   espresso
2 tbsp.   sugar
1 tbsp.   lecithin

PREPARATION OF ESPRESSO FOAM

1.   Combine all ingredients and heat until sugar is dissolved. Allow mixture to cool.

2.   Foam using a beater or a burr mixed at an angle. Spoon out the foam.

ASSEMBLE THE CAKE

1.   Once cakes have cooled, remove from pans and trim the tops to make them flat

2.   Cut each cake into 2 layers (4 total).

3.   Begin to build the cake by spreading the ganache on the first layer.

4.   Add the next layer of cake and spread with the peanut butter mousse.

5.   Add the next layer of cake and add the caramel.

6   Finally top it all off with the last layer of cake.

7.   Using half sheet pans punch out 4 9" circles as your cake layers.

8.   Upon completion use the espresso foam, peanut brittle and chocolate tuile to garnish the plate.

FREE RANGE CHICKEN
WITH ESCARGOT, GARLIC STUFFING, ACORN SQUASH AND VANILLA PARSLEY PISTOU

CHEF WILLIAM HOFFMAN

Serves: 4

PREPARATION OF CHICKENS

1. Take 2 whole free range chickens and quarter them, reserving thighs for another time

2. Fabricate breasts and legs. Trim all extra fat and sinew. French the leg bones.

3. Poach legs in enough duck fat to cover at 300 degrees for 2-3 hours until tender.

4. Make a pocket in the breast meat and stuff with 3 oz. of escargot and garlic stuffing. Tie with butchers twine. Roast stuffed breast at 400 degrees for approximately 20 minutes until internal temperature is 160 degrees. Let rest.

INGREDIENTS FOR ESCARGOT AND GARLIC STUFFING

4 oz.	onion (small dice)	**1 oz.**	olive oil
4 oz.	carrot (small dice)	**8 oz.**	French escargot (in brine)
½ oz.	shallots (minced)	**4 oz.**	brioche (cubed)
½ oz.	garlic (minced)	**¼ oz.**	fresh thyme (chopped)
1 oz.	white wine	**1 oz.**	unsalted butter
½ oz.	sherry vinegar	**salt and pepper to taste**	

PREPARATION FOR STUFFING

1. Sweat all vegetables in olive oil in a sauté pan until tender.

2. Deglaze with white wine and sherry vinegar. Add escargot and brioche. Season with salt and pepper, thyme and butter.

3. Cook until all liquid has been absorbed. Cool and reserve until ready to stuff the chicken breasts.

continued on page 118

RECIPE

Free Range Chicken...continued from page 117

INGREDIENTS FOR VANILLA PARSLEY PISTOU

2 oz.   parsley (picked)
2 oz.   spinach (picked)
I oz.   parmesan cheese
I clove   garlic
2 oz.   extra virgin olive oil
2 oz.   water (may need more when blending for consistency)
¼   fresh vanilla bean (split pod and scrape out with back of
               a knife), using only the beans. Reserve pod for other use.
salt and pepper to taste

PREPARATION FOR PISTOU

Put all ingredients into a blender. Blend until smooth. Adjust with water until a smooth consistency is reached. Reserve until plating.

PREPARATION FOR ACORN SQUASH

I.   Quarter I acorn squash, removing seeds. Drizzle with olive oil and season with salt and pepper.

2.   Roast acorn squash at 400 degrees for approximately 30-45 minutes until tender. Remove from oven and brush with I tbsp. melted butter.

GARNISHES

Escargot poached in butter
Parsley leaves
White truffle oil to drizzle
Sliced truffles (optional)
Fleur de sel (salt)
Vanilla froth

VANILLA FROTH PREPARATION

Whisk together until frothy:

¼ cup   milk
¼   fresh vanilla bean (beans only)
I tsp.   soy lecithin
I oz.   butter

ASSEMBLE ON PLATE:

Spoon vanilla parsley pistou onto plate. Slice chicken breast in half and arrange on top of the pistou. Place chicken leg and acorn squash on the plate. Garnish with vanilla froth, escargot poached in butter, parsley leaves, white truffle oil drizzles, sliced truffles and salt.

In the Orchard with the Rosazzas

As soon as there is the first fall chill in the morning air, is there anyone among us who isn't impatient go to head for the orchard for freshly picked apples or to pick our own? Or buy mums for fall decorating? Or pick out our pumpkins in anticipation of Halloween?

The Brandywine region is fortunate in having many great apple orchards that also serve as our fresh produce stands as well.

Our personal favorite is Glen Willow just outside Avondale and a few minutes from our house. We go there year around for produce, but we really love fall because Ella is an apple freak–tart and crispy–and because that is the time that families flock to the farm that occupies a quiet stretch of country lane between busy Routes 41 and 1.

The Rosazza family has been operating the orchard since 1955, although their roots in the area go back for more than 100 years. When we dropped by on a chilly fall weekend date to talk with the Rosazzas they were gathering in the last of their root crops from the field in preparation for winter.

It's a big operation, with 35 acres in apples (more than a dozen different varieties), another 12 in peaches and more than 60 acres in vegetables—the big draw for customers during the summer months.

Of course, we couldn't resist buying a peck of Winesaps, with Ella contentedly biting into one on the way home.

GLEN WILLOW ORCHARD | AVONDALE

610.268.8743

RECIPE

APPLESAUCE & RAISIN CAKE

ROSAZZA FAMILY RECIPE

"You can use canned applesauce for this recipe but why not fix fresh and homemade instead?"

INGREDIENTS

1 ¼ cup	flour
1 cup	sugar
¾ tsp.	baking soda
¾ tsp.	salt
¼ tsp.	baking powder
½ tsp.	cinnamon
¼ tsp.	cloves
¼ tsp.	allspice
¾ cup	applesauce
¼ cup	water
1	egg
½ cup	raisins
¼ cup	nuts
¼ cup	vegetable oil

PREPARATION

1. Preheat oven to 350 degrees.

2. Mix in bowl all dry ingredients, then blend in the remaining ingredients, stirring well.

3. Pour mixture into 9" by 9" inch greased baking pan and bake for 30-35 minutes

Can be served plain or with powder sugar or cream

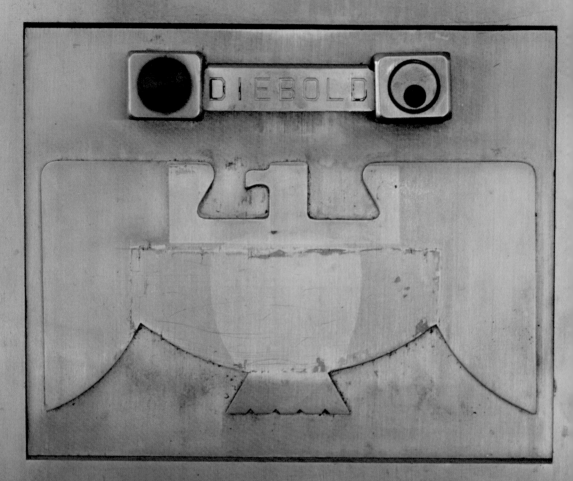

In West Grove, **Food on the Twelves**

*I*n France, every small town seems to have its own restaurant that, if not a Michelin one star, at least will have great food and a nonchalant atmosphere. Unfortunately, that is not generally the case in America, which is why it was so exciting to us locals to hear a couple of years ago that a new restaurant was opening in West Grove, 10 minutes from where we live.

For Tim and Kristin Smith, a young couple who had worked the kitchen and the front of the house, respectively, for most of their adult lives, the word "twelves" seemed to resonate in their lives. Their first date was November 12, both were born on a 12th (Tim on January 12, Kristin on February 12) and they wed on November 12. So even before they opened their first restaurant together, Twelves just seemed like the perfect name.

The Smiths came to West Grove for two reasons: They couldn't agree on terms and conditions at a building they had been pursuing elsewhere, and the right building opened up in West Grove with plenty of room, a central location and a past that was a good story. It was formerly a bank , opened in 1883 as the National Bank of West Grove. As Twelves is a BYOB, the old bank vault near the restaurant's entrance is now used for customer wine storage.

The restaurant is a little different in that it is open mornings as a coffee house, then morphs into an upscale grill for lunches and dinners.

Tim Smith's menu is in the bistro traditional with modern tweaks— hearty but never heavy. That's why his French onion soup and French-style steak frites are such great fare as we move into autumn.

TWELVES GRILL & CAFÉ | WEST GROVE
WWW.TWELVESGRILL.COM

RECIPE

FRENCH ONION SOUP

CHEF TIM SMITH

Serves: 4

INGREDIENTS

2	large yellow onion julienned
4 cups	beef stock
½ cup	Madeira wine
salt and pepper	
fresh thyme	
fresh parsley	
dried oregano	
I	sourdough baguette
¼ lb.	Provolone cheese
2 oz.	Asiago cheese

PREPARATION

1. In a large pot over low heat, sauté julienned onions until caramelized, giving them a deep brown color.

2. Deglaze the pan with Madeira and let simmer until reduced by half.

3. Add beef stock, chopped herbs, salt and pepper and let simmer for about 2-3 hours to fully absorb the sweet flavor of the onions. Add salt and pepper to taste.

3. Choose your favorite crusty bread, and cut into ½ inch croutons and toss with melted butter, salt and pepper, garlic powder and dried oregano. Bake croutons until crispy.

4. Pour soup in 4 heat-resistant cups and top with croutons then sliced Provolone and Asiago.

5. Place under broiler until charred.

Steak Frites with Red Wine Pan Sauce

RECIPE

Chef Tim Smith

Serves: 2

INGREDIENTS

8 oz.	beef loin, trimmed
I	Idaho potato
I	shallot, minced
3 oz.	red wine
3 oz.	beef stock
I gallon	peanut oil
½ tbsp.	butter

PREPARATION

1. Cut Idaho potato into ¼ inch sticks, and rinse in cold water and pat dry.

2. Bring peanut oil to 300 degrees. Carefully place fries in oil and blanch until barely soft—about 3 minutes. Place on cooling rack.

2. Increase heat of peanut oil to 375.

3. Heat sauté pan and add splash of olive oil. Season beef loin and sear in pan 2-3 minutes on each side, sealing in the juices and flavor. Remove beef from pan, going for a nice medium rare, set to rest to stop the juices from flowing to keep in the flavor in until cut.

4. To make a pan sauce, immediately add shallots to beef pan to caramelize beef juices, then add red wine to deglaze. Let simmer until reduced by half, add beef stock and simmer until deep brown and reduce by half. Whisk in butter, giving the sauce a syrupy consistency.

5. Place blanched fries back in oil and crisp about 2 minutes. Toss with salt and pepper, slice beef loin and drizzle pan sauce over beef.

Tailgating with the **Riabovs**

Tailgating—having a parking-area brunch and party with friends before any event—is most strongly associated with college football and is said to have originated with the Rutgers-Princeton game in 1869. "Tailgating" came with post-war station wagons, and when portable grills became popular in the '60s and '70s (remember hibachis?), tailgating quickly became a Saturday obsession from coast to coast.

John and Darelle Riabov have been tailgating at University of Delaware since they were married 22 years ago—sometimes at away games but mostly at Delaware Stadium in Newark. Both are U.D. grads—John, Class of '75 and Darelle, Class of '73—and Darelle is a former Blue Hen cheerleader and is now president of the alumni association.

Both John and Darelle are planners and pay attention to detail (he is an horologist, repairing timepieces large and small; she is a public relations and marketing exec at a healthcare firm), so their tailgaters are well-run so that the food is prepared on the spot and on time, and the cleanup done before the Alma Mater is sung.

John takes charge of food prep, and his go-to main dish is sailing eggs (a one-pan meal with ham, onions, potatoes) fixed from scratch at the stadium, which just happens to go well with his go-to drink, Bloody Marys made from scratch at home on game day. Darelle prefers baking, so dessert may be a slice of cake with fresh berries.

Of course, tailgating is a food event for all events in all seasons. Especially popular are tailgates before point-to-point horse races, a large regional sport in the mid-Atlantic states (copy that, Nebraska!). At these tailgaters—see our Spring section of this book—there are often style points not just for what you bring to the table, but also how many candelabra, floral arrangements and silver serving pieces are on that table.

So pull up a Bloody Mary or Mimosa and come join us.

JOHN & DARELLE RIABOV | LANDENBERG

RECIPE

SAILING EGGS

JOHN RIABOV

Serves: 6

INGREDIENTS

5 slices   bacon, cut in ½ inch slices
½   medium to large baking potato, washed (skin-on)
          and diced into small cubes
½   medium onion, diced
I doz.   Eggs

PREPARATION

1.   Cook bacon in 9" non-stick skillet until crisp and browned. Remove bacon from skillet and drain on paper towel. Leave about 1-2 tbsp. bacon fat in skillet and dispose of remaining bacon fat.

2. Add potatoes to skillet and cook until soft and lightly browned. Add onion to skillet and cook until translucent but not browned. Add bacon back to skillet.

3.   Break eggs into a bowl and beat with a fork or whisk to blend. Add beaten eggs to skillet with bacon, potatoes and onion and cook eggs to desired doneness.

4.   Salt and pepper to taste.

5.   Garnish plate with fresh fruit and serve with whole grain toast.

Jr's Blazing Bloody Marys

John Riabov

Serves: 8

INGREDIENTS FOR MIX

64 oz.	tomato juice
¾ tsp.	salt
1 ½ tsp.	celery seed
2 tbsp.	Worcestershire sauce
3 tbsp. plus	horseradish
7-9 drops	Tabasco red pepper sauce

PREPARATION

1. Mix all ingredients into the tomato juice.

2. Refrigerate for two days to allow the flavors to blend.

3. Serve in a tall glass mixed with a good quality vodka. Do not add ice.

4. Garnish with a lime wedge and celery stalk.

RECIPE

SOUR CREAM COFFEE CAKE

DARELLE RIABOV

Serves: 10

INGREDIENTS

1 cup	butter
3	eggs, separated
1 cup	granulated sugar
1 cup	dairy sour cream
1 ¾ cup	sifted flour
1 tsp.	baking soda
1 tsp.	baking powder

FOR TOPPING

¼ cup	granulated sugar
½ tsp.	cinnamon
½ cup	chopped pecans

PREPARATION

1. Cream butter and sugar in a bowl or mixer.

2. Add egg yolks and sour cream. Beat until light and fluffy.

3. Sift together dry ingredients and add to creamed mixture.

4. Beat egg whites separately until stiff. Fold in.

5. Pour batter into a greased and floured bundt pan.

6. Sprinkle with the topping and dot top with extra butter. Stir topping slightly into top of batter.

7. Bake at 325 degrees for 1 hour.

8. Allow to cool in pan for 15 minutes before turning out.

A Soufflé for Ella

For several years, Ella was one of those people who commuted almost daily to her job in New York—about a 2 ½ hour commute from our home to the Wilmington train station and then an early morning Amtrak to the city.

I did most of the cooking in those days, so when she got within about 10 minutes of home—where both a stop light and a small farm that raised llamas were located—she would call me on her cell phone to announce, "I'm at the llamas!" That was my signal to finish off whatever I was fixing and pour the wines.

After dinner, we would often take our wine outside to the hot tub where we might be dazzled by the nighttime stars or wear stocking caps when it was snowing.

But things don't always run smoothly on Amtrak, and Ella might call me to announce, "I'm not at the llamas. Our engine died outside of Trenton, and we're waiting for a replacement." One of those nights, I was making one of Ella's favorite dishes—a goat cheese soufflé—and she couldn't get enough "bars" on her cell to call me until I had just popped the soufflé into the oven.

I consider it one of my greatest accomplishments as a home cook that I cut back the oven to minimal heat and nursed the soufflé by dialing up and dialing down the temperature for an hour and a half until she got home.

She said it tasted wonderful—but what wouldn't after a long train delay?

Ella, this one's for you.

RECIPE

GOAT CHEESE SOUFFLÉ

ROGER MORRIS

"It's not important how high the soufflé rises, but it is important to have it creamy on the inside and crusty on the outside."

Serves: 4

INGREDIENTS

4 tbsp.	butter
4 tbsp.	white flour
I cup	milk
5	egg whites, whipped
4	egg yolks
2	4 oz. sections of chevre or goat cheese, preferably herbed

PREPARATION

1.   Preheat oven to 375 degrees.

2.   Over low heat, melt the butter in a large skillet that can hold all ingredients.

3.   Stir in the flour gradually, then the milk gradually until the mixture is smooth.

4.   Crumble the cheese into the mixture and stir until it has melted and become incorporated. Set aside.

5.   Separate the eggs and whip the whites until they start to hold peaks.

6.   The cheese mixture will have cooled sufficiently so you can first fold in the eggs yolks and then the egg whites.

7.   Spray a round ceramic soufflé dish with Pam. Pour in the mixture and bake for about 45 minutes or until the soufflé, which should have risen slightly, is turning a dark brown on top and has started to pull away from the sides of the dish.

8.   Serve immediately with Tomatoes and Artichoke Hearts Quick Stew on the side and some crusty bread.

TOMATOES & ARTICHOKE HEARTS QUICK STEW

RECIPE

ELLA MORRIS

This side dish adds some acidity and savory notes to balance the richness of the goat cheese soufflé.

Serves: 4

INGREDIENTS

I large can	whole tomatoes with basil
I small can	artichoke hearts
I cup	diced smoked ham or Canadian bacon
I	small onion, cut lengthwise

dried herbs de Provence and sea salt to taste

PREPARATION

I.   In a large skillet over moderate heat, sauté onions in light olive oil until soft.

2.   Add whole tomatoes, artichoke hearts and bacon and simmer 10-15 minutes until thoroughly heated but not boiling.

3.   Season and serve.

INDEX OF RECIPES

EAFOOD

SOUPS & STEWS

VEGETABLES